One Quilt
Many Pieces

One Quilt Many Pieces

A Guide to Mennonite Groups in Canada

Fourth Edition

Margaret Loewen Reimer

Foreword by James Urry

Herald Press
Waterloo, Ontario
Scottdale, Pennsylvania

Library and Archives Canada Cataloguing in Publication Data
Reimer, Margaret Loewen, 1947-
    One quilt many pieces : a guide to Mennonite groups in Canada / Margaret
Loewen Reimer.—4th ed.
    Includes bibliographical references.
    ISBN 978-0-8361-9405-0
1. Mennonites—Canada.   I. Title.
    BX8118.5.R45 2008
    289.7'71   C2007-906534-1

First Edition 1983
Second Edition 1984
Third Edition 1990
Fourth Edition 2008

The compilation of this book was supported by grants from
Mennonite Foundation of Canada
12 - 1325 Markham Road
Winnipeg, MB R3T 4J6
and

Mennonite Savings and Credit Union
1265 Strasburg Road
Kitchener, ON N2R 1S6

Bible text is from the *Revised Standard Version Bible*, Copyright © 1946, 1952,
1971, by the Division of Christian Education of the National Council of Churches
in the USA, and used by permission.

To my children: Christina, Thomas and Micah

Contents

Foreword

If there is one thing I have learned in over thirty years of studying Mennonites, it is that only a rash person ventures to generalize on the groups who make up the complex "Mennonite" world(s). Numerous reviewers of my writings, especially Mennonites, will gently remind readers of the review that my work does not include all Mennonite groups and will often list, in general terms, those I have overlooked or obviously chosen to exclude. The problem of too many names and too many varieties of Mennonites for any outsider to possibly comprehend is apparently long standing. In the early seventeenth century, the lawyer and humanist Hugo Grotius noted of the Dutch Mennonites that they possessed so many separate groups "that there is hardly anyone who knows their number, or all their names."

This Mennonite diversity is the product of time, space, and more recently, of evangelical activity. In terms of time and space, Mennonites have become a diverse people. With different points of origin, this diversity was exacerbated by subsequent divisions caused by internal divisions—some peaceful, others schismatically divisive—as well as by other circumstances such as forced and voluntary migration. In spite of this complex history of division, separation, and diaspora, few Mennonite groups ever completely lost touch with each other and, at least since the nineteenth century, there has been increasing contact and degrees of reintegration of the diverse groups. One aspect of this is the creation of institutions devoted to national and international cooperation. In the course of time, while groups and individuals have also flowed out of the movement, new individuals have also entered the Mennonite world, some more welcome than others. Since the nineteenth century, evangelical activities have brought new people and communities into the movement, some in distant lands from missionizing, others who have come from distant lands as immigrants to become friends, neighbours, and eventually fellow believers.

The term *Mennonite* was originally applied by outsiders to people and groups identified as the followers of one of the more noted founders, Menno Simons. As with Calvinists named after Jean Calvin and Lutherans after Martin Luther, the Mennonite name was at first applied by detractors. But in time it was appropriated by Mennonites, as were other identities derived from founders of groups spun off from the movement but never fully disconnected (Amish, Holdeman, and others). Some members of the evangelical wings often see the term *Mennonite* as a burden of history and have dropped the name. Others, entering the faith from outside the historical descent-line, have been quite willing to adopt it.

But there are other terms of identification that circulate within the Canadian Mennonite world that are also products of history but not necessarily of faith. These occasionally solidify into identities that rarely appear in conference names or on church notice boards. Some are repeatable; others are not. Mennonites identified as "Swiss" or "Swiss/South German" might well have been given their collective name by Mennonites from Russia who, in different migrations, designated each other with a variety of identifications. There once were the "Canadian (*Kanadier*)" and the "Russian (*Russlaender*)" Mennonites among those who came from Russia, although these terms too have shifted in their historical contexts and have become increasingly archaic. Some of these Mennonites have argued for a variety of national and racial connections outside the faith as Germans and Dutch, as Frisians, and even as Flemish. In recent times I have noticed a revolt by the descendants of the first immigrants from Russia, both against the term *Kanadier* and the more generic "Russian Mennonite" label. In its place the term "Low German Mennonites" has become popular, a title based on identification with a common patois in unspoken opposition to High German and perhaps even English. It is used to create a new linkage between Canadian Mennonites who migrated mainly from Canada to Mexico and Paraguay and onwards to Bolivia and Belize and other lands to the south of the 49th parallel.

So it is very helpful to have Margaret Loewen Reimer's account of the Canadian Mennonite worlds, thoroughly updated and providing both the confused outsider and the often equally confused insider with some guidance through this confused patchwork of identities. Readers should remember, however, that the patches actually hide an even longer labyrinth of thread that mysteriously connects the Mennonite worlds and precariously holds them together.

There I go, generalizing again.

James Urry
Victoria University of Wellington
New Zealand

Acknowledgments

Information for this book has been complied with the help of many church leaders, conference staff, archivists, and historians across the country. Thank-you to all those who provided statistics, checked facts, and offered suggestions. A special thank-you to historian John J. Friesen and archivists Sam Steiner and Conrad Stoesz for responding so promptly to my many questions. I also owe thanks to Tom Bender, who helped me sort out Swiss Conservative groups, and to Dean Martin, who provided supplementary information on Old Order communities, including a correction to media reports of a new Amish settlement in Manitoba—it is actually a settlement of Old Order Mennonites who wear Amish beards!

Thanks to staff from the Mennonite Brethren and Mennonite Church Canada offices for their help and to Terry Smith from the Evangelical Mennonite Conference and Lil Goertzen from the Evangelical Mennonite Mission Conference. Debbie Funk provided information on the Chortitzer Conference and Mal Braun on the Northwest Conference. The following assisted in gathering information on their groups: George Buhler, Bergthaler; Dick Schroeder, Sommerfelder; William Friesen, Reinland; Peter Wollf, Peter Elias, John Klassen, and Abe Harms, Old Colony; Wilhelm J. Thiessen, New Reinland; Marvin Penner, Church of God in Christ, Mennonite; Henry Unger, Milton Loewen, and Victor Dueck, Kleine Gemeinde; Joseph Stoll, Old Order Amish; Amsey Martin, Old Order Mennonite; Clare Frey, Markham-Waterloo; Melvin Roes, Beachy Amish.

Thanks to the Mennonite Foundation of Canada for a Legacy Grant and to Mennonite Savings and Credit Union for a project grant toward the writing of this book. Finally, thanks to Levi Miller at Herald Press for urging me to undertake this project and to *Canadian Mennonite* staff and board members for their support.

Preface

In 1981, as associate editor of the *Mennonite Reporter*, I began to compile information for a series of articles on Mennonite groups in Canada. It was an appropriate venture for the *Reporter*, which was an independent, inter-Mennonite tabloid seeking to report on the variety of groups and individuals that make up the Mennonite mosaic in this country. While some groups defied neat classification, the series gave a fairly accurate picture of how Mennonite churches have organized themselves in Canada. The articles appeared in the *Mennonite Reporter* between November 9, 1981, and May 31, 1982.

In 1983, I updated the information and compiled the series for a book entitled *One Quilt, Many Pieces: A Reference Guide to Mennonite Groups in Canada*. The book was published by the Mennonite Publishing Service, publisher of the *Mennonite Reporter*. A slightly revised edition was published in 1984. The third edition, substantially revised and reorganized, was launched at the Mennonite World Conference Assembly in Winnipeg in 1990. A new edition is long overdue.

When I left my editorial position at the *Canadian Mennonite* (successor to the *Mennonite Reporter*) in 2005, I set aside time to update this book. Assisted by grants from the Mennonite Foundation of Canada and the Mennonite Savings and Credit Union in Ontario, I set to work gathering statistics and documenting changes in the Mennonite church scene since 1990. One of the most dramatic changes I experienced this time around was having the internet at my fingertips. It is astonishing how much detail on Mennonites is available online. For this book, however, I decided not to list website addresses, except for major online resources such as the Global Anabaptist Mennonite Encyclopedia Online (www.gameo.org). Information on specific Mennonite groups and institutions can easily be found through any search engine.

There are various ways one could organize the list of Mennonite groups in Canada. The first edition of this book began with the Old Order groups and moved through groupings of conservative and mainstream churches, ending with the two largest denominations. The 1990 edition began with the largest groups and then listed the others by size and geographical spread, disregarding historical connections. This new edition pays more attention to historical context and links between groups.

The first section includes the two largest national denominations—the

Preface Ⓐ   B (Mine)

Canadian Conference of Mennonite Brethren Churches and Mennonite
Church Canada—along with two other multi-province conferences. All
four of these church bodies are active in inter-Mennonite activities and participate in Mennonite World Conference. The two regional conferences
next in the book, one based in Manitoba and one in Alberta, stand somewhere between the groups in the first section and the conservative groups *Mine*
in theology and lifestyle.

Conservative bodies are grouped according to their Russian or Swiss
origins because those origins still define in significant ways who they are
today. While some of these groups continue to identify themselves as
German-speaking church communities (*Gemeinden*), this book uses the
English names for the benefit of readers. Old Order communities precede
Swiss Conservatives in the book because they were established long before
the conservative churches came into being. The last section includes two
groups related to Mennonites: The Brethren in Christ are partners in
Mennonite World Conference and Mennonite Central Committee; the
Hutterian Brethren are linked to Mennonites by their history and commu-
nal values, although there are no organizational ties.

The appendices include a membership summary, a list of Mennonite
organizations and schools, and information on the worldwide Mennonite
church. A "family tree" charts the lineage of the various groups from the
time of arrival in Canada. The bibliography provides resources for further
study and a sample of the rich field of Mennonite literature in Canada.

Margaret Loewen Reimer
October 2007

Introduction

The quilt is an apt symbol for Mennonites. Quilting, of course, has long been associated with certain Mennonite and Amish groups. The patchwork quilt is particularly appropriate because it includes a diversity of colours and fabrics and textures, all stitched together in a traditional pattern to make a serviceable cover. The diversity of pieces in the Mennonite quilt is a striking feature of this book.

Mennonites first arrived in Canada in 1786 and settled in the Niagara Peninsula of Ontario, then known as Upper Canada. Coming from Pennsylvania, they were descendants of Swiss/South German Anabaptists who had fled Europe in the late 1600s to seek religious freedom in the United States. These "Swiss Mennonites" were joined in Canada by their Amish cousins who emigrated directly from Europe beginning in 1822. (There is some speculation that Mennonites came to the Atlantic provinces from the United States in the mid-1700s, but there are no records to verify this.) By 1841, there were about 5,000 Mennonites in Ontario.

Mennonites with quite a different history began arriving on the Canadian prairies in 1874, about 7,000 of them by 1880. These were people of Dutch/North German background whose ancestors had moved to Poland and Prussia and then to Russia before coming to Canada. Another 18,000 of these "Russian Mennonites" came to Canada in the 1920s, and another 7,700 after World War II.

All the Mennonite groups described in this book have emerged from these two immigrant streams. *Swiss* and *Russian* Mennonite are simply catch-all terms to distinguish between the two historical groups, which developed theologically and culturally in rather different ways. While these terms do not apply to nearly all Mennonites in Canada today, they are still useful for situating and organizing current groups in order to understand them better. One of the defining characteristics of Mennonites historically is their sense of peoplehood, not in ethnic terms per se but in the sense of an organic community shaped by the integration of theology, culture, and lifestyle. Not unlike the Jews, Mennonites can be understood as a "culture of faith," as James Urry calls it in his book *Mennonites, Politics, and Peoplehood* (University of Manitoba Press, 2006).

Over the years, of course, people from a wide variety of ethnic and cultural backgrounds have joined Mennonite churches, and some have built their own ethnic congregations within the Mennonite fold. The two largest denominations—the Canadian Conference of Mennonite Brethren Churches and Mennonite Church Canada—include German- and French-speaking congregations alongside immigrant congregations that worship in Hispanic, Chinese, Korean, Vietnamese, Arabic, and Punjabi, among other languages. The conservative and Old Order groups remain much more homogeneous, many still worshipping in the German dialects of their ancestors.

Mennonite churches in Canada today have a total of 122,858 baptized members, according to 2006 statistics compiled for this book. This is a conservative number, based on available figures from identifiable groups and does not include children, or adults who identify themselves as Mennonites by heritage but are not church members. (See Appendix 1.) In the 2001 Canadian census, 191,470 people identified themselves as Mennonite, making up 0.6 percent of the Canadian population, just below Greek Orthodox and Sikhs. (See Appendix 3.)

Most of the churches are located in five provinces (British Columbia to Ontario). There are about twelve Mennonite congregations in Quebec and a few in Nova Scotia and New Brunswick, including several Conservative Russian Mennonite communities that have moved there from South America in recent decades. This book identifies about twenty distinct church groups, plus various subgroups and independent congregations that come under the Mennonite umbrella. These range from national denominations to informal fellowships, from multi-staff corporations to small communities of congregations (*Gemeinden*) led by one bishop.

Why are there so many different groups? For a relatively small membership, Mennonites have produced a surprising (some would say shocking) number of church organizations. How did this happen? The answer lies not only within a turbulent history but also in the very fundamentals of the Mennonite faith.

A History of Migration

The Mennonite church has its roots in the Reformation of sixteenth-century Europe and is often called its "radical" wing. While reformers such as Martin Luther and John Calvin called for change in the Catholic Church, others protested that Luther and Calvin did not go far enough. These protesters challenged fundamental practices such as infant baptism, the unity of church and state, and the authority of priests. In 1525, radicals in southern Europe, who called themselves Swiss Brethren, rebaptized each other to publicize their belief that church membership should be voluntary and the church distinct from the rest of the world. Others followed suit, giving rise to the name Anabaptists (rebaptizers). In 1536, a Dutch priest named Menno Simons joined the Anabaptist movement, spending the rest of his life ministering to fledgling congregations and articulating a theology to guide them. Under his leadership, Anabaptists became known as Mennists or Mennonites.

Anabaptist-Mennonites refused to participate in the military or swear oaths of loyalty to any earthly leader. While acknowledging the right of the state in civil matters, they insisted that the church's primary loyalty is to the rule of Christ. That rule is guided by the Bible, as interpreted by one's conscience and tested within the community of faith. In other words, authority for the Anabaptists was based on communal rather than priestly authority and on the Bible rather than tradition. While they differed on the degree to which they should participate in civil life, Anabaptists agreed that their churches were not answerable to the state. This stance obviously threatened the established authorities and resulted in the imprisonment and martyrdom of many Anabaptists in the first century of the movement. Many fled their homes in search of a place to live out their faith in peace.

In 1693, the Swiss Brethren Anabaptists in the Alsace region experienced disagreements over church discipline and nonconformity to the world. Jakob Ammann, a leader who argued for a stricter discipline, left with his followers and began a new church. Ammann's group became known as Amish Mennonite or simply Amish. (An earlier division, in 1533, resulted in the Hutterite movement, which has developed independently from the Mennonites.)

Groups of Dutch Mennonites began seeking shelter in Poland and later Prussia beginning in the 1540s. In the late 1780s, many of these settlers answered Catherine the Great's invitation to form agricultural colonies in southern Russia and the Ukraine.

Meanwhile, a few Dutch Mennonites found their way to North America. There is evidence of Dutch Mennonites in Manhattan as early as 1644; in 1663 one of them established a communal settlement along the Delaware River, later destroyed by British troops. The major migration of Mennonites to North America began in 1683, when a group from Krefeld, Germany, decided to join Quaker William Penn's experiment in brotherly love in Pennsylvania. They settled in Germantown (now part of Philadelphia), where they founded the first Mennonite congregation in North America, a congregation still in existence. The stone meetinghouse built in 1770 to replace the first log structure is now a historic site. The group from Krefeld was soon followed by about 4,000 Swiss and South German Mennonites, as well as some 200 Amish, who settled in eastern Pennsylvania.

After the American Revolution, some of these settlers in Pennsylvania decided to come to Canada, joining a stream of United Empire Loyalists who wanted to live under the British monarchy. The first Mennonite congregation in Canada, appropriately named The First Mennonite Church, was established in 1801 in Vineland, Ontario, by these Swiss Mennonites from Pennsylvania. Today this congregation is a member of Mennonite Church Canada.

Nonconformity and Division

The history of persecution and migration has played a large role in shaping Mennonite identity. Seeking freedom to worship in peace, Mennonites formed communities outside mainstream society and largely kept to themselves. (An exception were those who remained in the Netherlands and came to play leading roles in that country's Golden Age of art and commerce in the 1600s.) This enforced isolation from society became fused with the theological conviction that Christians are called out of "the world" and into a holy community under God's rule, based on biblical texts such as "come out from them, and be separate" (2 Corinthians 6:17), and "do not be conformed to this world" (Romans 12:2). Thus Mennonites developed a separatist and sectarian psychology or self-understanding. While for some this meant living simple, upright lives amid their worldly neighbours, Mennonites in Russia created their own self-governed colonies with their own schools, hospitals, and economic institutions, a model they brought to Canada. Hutterites were the only group that retained the Anabaptist ideal of establishing communities that hold all things in common.

This sense of being set apart, a holy people under the rule of Christ, is at the heart of Mennonite self-identity. It is what drives the Mennonite quest for ethical purity and true Christian community.

The obsession with ethical purity and nonconformity to the world is both the genius and the most vulnerable part of the Mennonite faith. One could say it is the Achilles heel within the Mennonite peace position, for the quest for a church "without spot or wrinkle" (Ephesians 5:27) has led to bitter conflicts and divisions through the centuries, setting member against member and leader against leader in the struggle to determine "God's will." Communal authority does not always exist peacefully with a commitment to individual conscience, and a church polity based on "the priesthood of all believers" (Luther's phrase that has become a Mennonite byword) cannot function harmoniously without good leadership. Mennonite history bears witness to the dangers of sectarian idealism: the obsession with nonconformity and faithful discipleship has often degenerated into harsh intolerance and exclusion from the group, leaving behind a fragmented body with each part claiming to know the true way. The Mennonite heritage quilt includes some clashing colours and ragged edges that remain visible to this day.

Given this divisive history, it is no surprise that the groups in this book represent a broad range of convictions on what it means to live faithfully within Canadian culture. The more conservative groups are intent on conserving the traditions, both religious and cultural, that have kept them separate from the rest of society. Their emphasis on nonconformity often includes distinctive dress and head coverings for women, a suspicion of higher education, and a simple, rural lifestyle. The most radical nonconformists, the Old Order Mennonites and Amish, are also the most visible: no one can miss their distinctiveness as they ride by in their horse-drawn buggies, clothed in sober, nineteenth-century garb.

The sense of the church as a separate community that encompasses all aspects of life is still evident in these conservative groups. For example, in my research for this book I was amazed at the detailed directories published by Old Order and conservative churches, listing the names of every family member, dates of baptism, marriages, and even occupations. These directories are obviously not for outsiders—they contain no description of the group or its beliefs—they are meant simply "to keep us in touch with each other, and to get to know each other better" (*Directory of the Markham-Waterloo Mennonite Congregations*). This emphasis on family and caring for each other gets to the heart of a communal identity, but it also tends to fix group boundaries, to clarify who is in and who is out.

Less conservative Mennonite groups, especially the two largest, have gradually laid aside their sectarian and cultural distinctives, though not with out controversy, as they have become established welcomed newcomers into their midst. Mission e turies have seen Mennonite churches established Mennonite World Conference, to which four Can. now encompasses almost 1.5 million members in 7 6 for membership summary).

Foundations of Faith

Despite ongoing differences in theology, worship, lifestyle, and accommodation to culture, one can still see evidence of the foundation—the traditional pattern of the quilt—laid at the beginning of the Anabaptist-Mennonite movement. This foundation includes the primary authority of the biblical Word, adult baptism, discipleship (following Jesus in daily life), and an emphasis on community and service. While worship styles differ greatly, all the groups in this book observe the two Mennonite ordinances of Baptism and the Lord's Supper. (For a time, Swiss Mennonites had five additional ordinances—foot washing, marriage, prayer coverings for women, anointing, and the holy kiss—but the primary ones were always Baptism and the Lord's Supper.) For Mennonites, these acts are not sacraments in the Catholic sense of being actual means of God's grace; they are signs of our response to that grace. Baptism is a sign of a person's decision to accept God's saving grace through Christ by becoming a member of the church, Christ's visible body on earth. The Lord's Supper, or Communion, is observed in remembrance of Christ's death.

The commitment to nonviolence is probably the most distinguishing feature of the Mennonite faith. "The regenerated do not go to war, nor engage in strife," said Menno Simons. Christians are called to turn the other cheek, as Jesus taught, to die rather than resist. Martyrdom was often the result of this nonresistance in the early years of Anabaptism. Over the centuries, Mennonites have differed on how nonresistant they should be and when to resist injustice and seek to influence governments, but their corporate commitment to nonviolence has remained firm. This core belief of the Mennonite confession of faith, which includes objection to military service, marks Mennonites as one of the Historic Peace Churches, along with the Society of Friends (Quakers) and the Church of the Brethren, an American denomination with German Pietist and Anabaptist roots.

The Canadian government from the beginning promised Mennonites exemption from military service, although not all have taken that exemption. In World War I, Mennonites and others could register as conscientious objectors (COs) to participation in the military. In World War II, Mennonite groups joined hands to persuade the government to establish an alternative service program for COs. Hundreds of men served in CO camps in the Canadian wilderness, planting trees and building roads for the duration of the war.

Throughout history, the Mennonite propensity for division has been ed by an impulse to reunite with like-minded believers and to join in efforts to help others. Recent decades have seen the merger of two major Mennonite denominations, resulting in Mennonite Church Canada, as well as alliances among conservative groups with very different histories, such as Old Colony Russian Mennonites and Swiss Conservatives. The two largest groups in Canada, descendants of a bitter division in Russia in 1860, united their church colleges in Winnipeg in 1999 to create Canadian Mennonite University. Other groups have also joined in educational efforts, including training for pastors.

The most unifying force among Mennonites is undoubtedly the imperative to help the less fortunate. Most of the groups described in this book work together to provide aid and assist victims of disaster, most notably through Mennonite Central Committee (MCC) and Mennonite Disaster Service (MDS). Locally and regionally, the traditional commitment to mutual aid has led to cooperation in establishing schools, homes for seniors, programs for mentally ill and disabled people, medical facilities including a hospital (Concordia Hospital in Winnipeg was begun by Mennonites in 1928), and financial institutions. (See Appendix 5 for a list of inter-Mennonite organizations.)

Beginning with church funds for their own needy members, Mennonites in Canada have developed a network of financial services, including insurance companies, credit unions, and investment services. While many of these institutions now serve a broader public, some retain a distinctly Mennonite identity. The Mennonite Foundation of Canada, which serves a variety of Mennonite groups, manages members' investments for charitable purposes and provides stewardship education for churches. The Mennonite Savings and Credit Union in Ontario serves exclusively members of Mennonite and Brethren in Christ churches, including the Old Order communities. MAX Canada provides insurance services to members of the wider Anabaptist community (extending to Hutterites and Quakers), building on an Ontario Mennonite aid program founded in 1866. Through Mennonite Economic Development Associates, Mennonite business and professional people share their skills and their wealth with people in many countries.

The quilting image again comes to mind. Essentially a practical skill for the home, quilting at its best becomes an art form valued in the public sphere. So too with these other "domestic skills" often associated with Mennonites, such as mutual aid, hard work, and nonviolence. Nurtured in close (often closed) communities, these Mennonite "arts" are today making a significant impact, both practical and theological, in settings far beyond their own communities.

One Quilt, Many Pieces

The Mennonite quilt is indeed a patchwork of many pieces and textures. I hope this book helps to bring out the colour of each piece and to reveal the underlying pattern that unites them.

A Mennonite Glossary

Amish: An offshoot of the Anabaptists, the Amish are named after Jakob Ammann, who left the Swiss Brethren Anabaptists in 1693 to form his own church. In Canada, the only group to retain this name is the Old Order Amish.

Anabaptists: Meaning "rebaptizers," this term was applied in the sixteenth century to the radical reformers who baptized adults into a "free" church separate from the state. Today the term is used in three ways: (1) to refer to the beginnings of the Mennonite movement, (2) as interchangeable with *Mennonite*, and (3) to refer to churches outside the European Mennonite tradition that identify with Anabaptist values.

Church/Conference: *Church* can mean both a congregation and a group of related congregations (the German *Gemeinde* means both "church" and "community"). A conference is an organization with member congregations. While Mennonites as a whole are sometimes called a denomination, that term is also applied to the larger groups within the Mennonite fold, such as Mennonite Church Canada.

Conservatives: This term applies to Mennonite groups intent on "conserving" or maintaining traditional distinctives, such as head coverings for women and avoidance of popular culture. Swiss Conservatives tend to mix nonconformity with evangelical emphases.

Low German: A language of the lowlands of northern Europe that Dutch Mennonites adopted when they moved to Poland and Prussia and later to Russia. Because these Mennonites lived in relative isolation, they developed a distinctive "Mennonite Low German," which they brought to Canada and Latin America.

Mennonites: The name comes from Menno Simons, a leader of the Anabaptists in Holland in the sixteenth century. Today that name applies to the worldwide church body that grew out of those Reformation roots.

Old Order: These are the "horse and buggy" Mennonites and Amish, the m̲ nal of all Mennonite groups. They have resisted modernization retain a simple, rural way of life and traditional religious

utch: The German dialect (*Dutch* is an aberration of to Swiss and South German immigrants, not only Mennonites, who moved to Pennsylvania and later to Ontario.

Russian Mennonites: A popular name for Anabaptist-Mennonites origi-
nating in Holland who moved to Poland and Prussia and then to southern
Russia/Ukraine before coming to Canada in the late nineteenth century.

Swiss Mennonites: A popular name for Anabaptist-Mennonites origi-
nating in Switzerland and South Germany who moved to Pennsylvania
in the early 1700s and then to Ontario beginning in 1786. They have
also been known as "Old Mennonites" in contrast to the "newer"
immigrants such as the Russian Mennonites.

1
Largest Multi-province Conferences

Choral music is an important part of Mennonite life in Canada. The Winnipeg Mennonite Children's Choir is an internationally recognized choir founded by Helen Litz. Other well-known children's groups include the Pacific Mennonite Children's Choir founded by Nancy Dyck in 1978 in Abbotsford, British Columbia, and the Inter-Mennonite Children's Choir, founded in 1967 in Waterloo, Ontario. Longstanding adult choirs include the Faith and Life Male Choir, a ministry of Mennonite Church Manitoba, and the West Coast Mennonite Chamber Choir, whose CD sales support Mennonite Central Committee programs in British Columbia.

This section begins with the two major Mennonite denominations in Canada: the Canadian Conference of Mennonite Brethren Churches and Mennonite Church Canada. These are by far the largest Mennonite church bodies in this country, with national offices as well as regional organizations. The two other groups—the Evangelical Mennonite Conference and the Evangelical Mennonite Mission Conference—also span several provinces.

The two largest groups could be called "mainstream" denominations: members live their faith within the world, active in the business, professional, and political life of Canada; they participate in ecumenical activities and in witness beyond their borders; they welcome members from many backgrounds and cultures. In Mennonite Church Canada, the regional bodies are partners with the national church, operating their own institutions and programs while contributing to the work of the Canadian body. The Mennonite Brethren provincial conferences operate their own schools and camps.

Student chapel at Conrad Grebel University College at the University of Waterloo. The chapel's beautiful stained glass windows were designed by Nancy Lou Patterson, a former fine arts professor at the university.

Both the Mennonite Brethren conference and Mennonite Church Canada maintain ties with their counterparts in the United States, cooperating in seminary education, international ministries, and publishing of church resources. Both groups recently ended publication of their German periodicals, due to dwindling readership. *Die Mennonitische Rundschau* (1880-2007) had been a Mennonite Brethren magazine since 1945. *Der Bote* (1924-2008) was a periodical of Mennonite Church Canada.

The two smaller groups—Evangelical Mennonite Conference and Evangelical Mennonite Mission Conference—while more separate from the mainstream, have much in

Horseback riding at Camp Assiniboia near Winnipeg.

common with the larger groups. They cooperate in Mennonite activities beyond their own churches, including education and service. They participate in the global church through Mennonite World Conference, and their mission programs relate to the Council of International Anabaptist Ministries. All four of these groups have head offices in Manitoba.

In the last two decades, a number of congregations have left Mennonite Church Canada and its provincial bodies over theological differences. These are listed in the membership summary (Appendix 1) as independent congregations. The three congregations in Alberta have about 430 members. Rosemary Mennonite Church, with about 200 members, belongs to Mennonite Church Alberta but not to Mennonite Church Canada, so its membership is included here as well. Of the two congregations that left Mennonite Church British Columbia recently, one joined the Mennonite Brethren; the other is independent, with about 95 members. Three congregations in Manitoba have about 400 members. Of the seven congregations that left Mennonite Church Saskatchewan, two no longer identify themselves as Mennonite. The other five congregations have about 885 members.

The annual Canada Day Celebration at Killarney Park Mennonite Brethren Church in Vancouver shows "our church community at play with the neighbourhood," according to pastor Ken Peters.

The campus of Columbia Bible College in Abbotsford, BC. The college, which had 535 students in 2007, is operated jointly by the BC Conference of Mennonite Brethren Churches and Mennonite Church BC.

Candian Conference of Mennonite Brethren Churches

The CANADIAN CONFERENCE
of Mennonite Brethren Churches

Members	36,843
Congregations	248

Location
In 8 provinces

Head office
1310 Taylor Avenue
Winnipeg, MB R3M 3Z6

Schools
Mennonite Brethren Biblical
Seminary (in partnership with
U.S. Conference of Brethren
Churches, with Canada teach-
ing centres in Winnipeg and
in ACTS seminary group at
Trinity Western University,
British Columbia)

Institutions
Centre for Mennonite Brethren
Studies
Christian Press
Kindred Productions (with U.S.
conference)
MBMS International (mission
partnership with U.S. confer-
ence), with head office in
Abbotsford, British Columbia,
and regional office in Winnipeg

Periodicals
Mennonite Brethren Herald
Le Lien, Chinese Herald
Mennonite Historian (newsletter
of Centre for MB Studies and
Mennonite Heritage Centre of
Mennonite Church Canada)
Direction (journal of MB post-
secondary schools in North
America)

History

The Mennonite Brethren church was born in Russia in 1860 when a renewal movement swept through the Mennonite communities there. Those urging renewal complained that the church in the Mennonite colonies had taken on the character of a state church: lines between religious and civic authority were blurred, church membership was a prerequi-site for civic privileges such as land owner-ship, and moral decadence went unpunished. They were convinced that the church was in a state of dead formalism and spiritual stag-nation.

The greatest catalyst for renewal was a German Pietist pastor, Eduard Wuest, who attracted people with his powerful preaching and vibrant spirituality. A number of Men-nonites experienced dramatic conversions, and these "brethren," as they called themselves, began to meet in homes for Bible study and prayer. They took communion without church leaders' approval and challenged the spiritual authority of the mother church. Efforts to dis-cipline this renegade church turned into a pro-tracted and bitter dispute.

In January 1860, 27 brethren signed a letter explaining their differences with the established church and withdrawing their membership. The new Mennonite Brethren church that they formed emphasized personal conversion and baptism by immersion. By 1872, the Mennonite Brethren church numbered about 600 members. Evangelism was a priority, and the church was soon involved in foreign missions.

From 1874 to 1880, many Mennonite Brethren joined the move to North America, prompted by economic factors and the Russian government's plans to introduce universal military service. The Mennonite Brethren settled in the midwestern United States and were soon organizing mission endeavours. These included evangelism efforts among Russian Mennonites who had settled in Manitoba. In 1883, two Mennonite Brethren ministers were sent to win converts among the Old Colony Mennonite settlers in Manitoba who were reportedly receiving little spiritual guidance from their leaders.

The first Mennonite Brethren (MB) church in Canada was established in 1888 near Winkler, Manitoba, by converts from the Old Colony. Mennonite Brethren who moved to Saskatchewan from the United States also formed several congregations after 1895. The beginning of the Canadian MB conference can be traced to 1910, when 13 churches formed the northern district of the North American MB church.

The Canadian church grew rapidly with the coming of 18,000 Russian Mennonites to Canada between 1923 and 1927, about a quarter of them Mennonite Brethren. More immigrants came from Europe after World War II.

The Canadian Conference of the Mennonite Brethren in North America was established in 1945. This new structure made church growth and evan-

The Westwood Community Church is a Mennonite Brethren congregation in Winnipeg. The building is one of several churches designed by Mennonite architect Harold Funk.

When He comes, our glorious King
All His ransomed home to bring
Then anew this song we'll sing
Hallelujah! What a Saviour!

Singers lead the congregation in worship at the Waterloo Mennonite Brethren Church in Ontario.

gelism, youth work, Christian education, and higher education the responsibility of the national conference. The conference absorbed two smaller groups that had been associated with the Mennonite Brethren: the *Allianz Gemeinde* (Alliance Church) and the Krimmer Mennonite Brethren Church. The Allianz had been organized in Russia in 1905 to bridge differences between the Mennonite Brethren and the larger Mennonite church. When the Allianz joined the Canadian MB conference, its inclusiveness was tempered, particularly with regard to baptism (the MB church accepted only immersion baptism). The Krimmer church, which emerged from the *Kleine Gemeinde* in the Russian Crimea (Krim) in 1869, merged with the MB conference in 1960.

The Canadian MB conference established Mennonite Brethren Bible College in Winnipeg in 1944, building on a tradition of Bible schools founded earlier by provincial congregations. (This college, later called Concord College, is now part of Canadian Mennonite University.) The conference began mission work in Quebec and Atlantic Canada in the 1960s, and later among various ethnic groups across Canada. Currently, congregations in eight provinces worship in about 17 languages.

Institutions located in Winnipeg include the Centre for Mennonite Brethren Studies, Christian Press, and Kindred Productions, the publisher for the North American Mennonite Brethren church. The Canadian conference continues to partner with the U.S. Conference of Mennonite Brethren Churches in three areas: (1) seminary education through Mennonite Brethren Biblical Seminary in Fresno, California, (2) mission work through Mennonite Brethren Mission and Service International, which has workers in over 60 countries, and (3) the Mennonite Brethren Historical Commission. The conference is a member of Mennonite Central Committee and other inter-Mennonite organizations, including Mennonite World Conference. It is also a member of the Evangelical Fellowship of Canada.

Distinctives

The mission statement of the Mennonite Brethren conference is, "Healthy, growing churches reaching their worlds." Its three priorities are reaching out to spiritually lost people in Canada and beyond with the healing gospel of Christ, leadership development, and healthy churches. Sometimes identifying itself as "Evangelical Anabaptist," the Mennonite Brethren church emphasizes personal salvation and evangelical piety, discipleship, knowledge of the Bible, covenant community, outreach, and peacemaking.

A focus on conversion and baptism by immersion initially distinguished Mennonite Brethren from other Mennonite groups. Today, the Mennonite Brethren church has much in common with mainstream evangelicalism, including contemporary worship styles and child evangelism programs, which may explain the young age of some baptismal candidates: 2005 statistics showed 17 baptisms of children 11 years and younger. British Columbia, which has over 50 percent of the national membership, has several "megachurches," with multiple staff and programs. Willingdon MB Church in Burnaby, for example, has 2,040 members (with Sunday attendance of over 3,000) and ministries in eight languages.

The conference is organized in two main boards: the Executive Board and the Board of Faith and Life. The ministries are divided into six services: church health, developing leaders, multiplying churches, communications, financial ministries, and upholding biblical and ethical integrity (Faith and Life). In 2006, after many years of debate, the conference opened all levels of pastoral leadership to women.

Mennonite Brethren Provincial Conferences

The six provincial conferences each have their own staff and boards, and operate programs in church planting, camping, youth ministry, Christian education, and other areas. The provincial bodies oversee ordination of pastors and provide resources for pastors and congregations. Congregations also relate to a variety of church-related institutions and programs in their regions.

Alberta Conference of MB Churches

Members	2,632
Congregations	27

Founded: 1928

School: Bethany College, Hepburn, Saskatchewan (in partnership with the Saskatchewan MB Conference and Evangelical Mennonite Mission Conference of Saskatchewan)

Camp: Camp Evergreen

British Columbia Conference of MB Churches

Members	19,376
Congregations	106
(1 dually affiliated with Mennonite Church British Columbia)	

Founded: 1931

Schools: Columbia Bible College (in partnership with Mennonite Church British Columbia)

Relates to Mennonite Educational Institute (K-12 school supported by 14 congregations)

Camps: Stillwood Camp, Gardom Lake Bible Camp, Pines Bible Camp, Campfire Ministries

Manitoba Conference of MB Churches

Members	6,439
Congregations	38
(1 dually affiliated with Mennonite Church Manitoba)	

Founded: 1929

Schools: Mennonite Brethren Collegiate Institute (grades 6-12)

Canadian Mennonite University (in partner-

33

ship with Mennonite Church Canada)
The Winnipeg Centre for Ministry Studies (a partnership of 4 schools and 5 Manitoba Mennonite conferences)
Institutions: Family Life Network (media production agency)
Camp: Simonhouse Bible Camp

Ontario Conference of MB Churches

Members	4,269
Congregations	32

Founded: 1932
Schools: Eden High School (now a public school; MB conference provides Bible teachers and board members)
Institutions: Tabor Manor (home for seniors)
Bethesda Home (home for mentally disabled)
Camp: Camp Crossroads

Quebec Conference of MB Churches (L'Association des Églises des Frères Mennonites du Québec)

Members	493
Congregations	10

Founded: 1982
School: Montreal Evangelical School of Theology (École de Théologie Évangélique de Montréal)
Camp: Camp Péniel

Saskatchewan Conference of MB Churches

Members	3,415
Congregations	30

Founded: 1946
School: Bethany College (in partnership with Alberta MB conference and Evangelical Mennonite Mission Conference of Saskatchewan)
Camps: Redberry Bible Camp, West Bank Bible Camp

Atlantic Provinces

Members	219
Congregations	5

3 congregations in New Brunswick, 2 in Nova Scotia

Mennonite Church Canada

Members	33,464

Congregations	224

Location
In 7 provinces

Head office
600 Shaftesbury Blvd.
Winnipeg, MB R3P 0M4

Schools
Associated Mennonite Biblical
  Seminary (in partnership with
  Mennonite Church USA)
Canadian Mennonite University
  (in partnership with Manitoba
  Conference of Mennonite
  Brethren Churches)
Relates officially to Conrad
  Grebel University College,
  Columbia Bible College, and
  Canadian Association of
  Mennonite Schools

Institutions
Mennonite Heritage Centre
  (Archives and Art Gallery)
Resource Centre
Mennonite Publishing Network
  (in partnership with Mennonite
  Church USA)

Periodicals
World of Witness (directory of
  workers)
Canadian Mennonite (official
  magazine)
Intotemak (Native Ministry
  newsletter)
Mennonite Historian (newsletter
  of Mennonite Heritage Centre
  and Centre for Mennonite
  Brethren Studies)

Mennonite Church Canada

History

Mennonite Church Canada came into being in 1999, a result of the union of two large North American church bodies: the Mennonite Church and the General Conference Mennonite Church. The Mennonite Church had included three regional Canadian conferences founded by members of Swiss and Amish background: the Mennonite Conference of Ontario and Quebec, the Western Ontario Mennonite Conference, and the Northwest Mennonite Conference based in Alberta. The General Conference included the Conference of Mennonites in Canada, founded by Russian Mennonites in 1903. (Members of the Mennonite Church were often called "Old Mennonites" to distinguish them from the newer General Conference and from the more recent immigrants from Russia, who identified with the General Conference.)

Canadian church leaders were at the forefront of the decision in 1999 not only to merge but also to form separate Canadian and U.S. bodies. And so Mennonite Church Canada was born, a union of the three historic streams of immigration: Swiss, Amish, and Russian Mennonite. (The Northwest Conference decided not to join Mennonite Church Canada and is now independent.)

The two Ontario-based conferences named above had already integrated with their Russian Mennonite sister conference in Ontario in 1988. This integrated body, with

Women at First Hmong Mennonite Church in Kitchener worship in their native Lao dress.

about 14,000 members and 90 congregations, called itself the Mennonite Conference of Eastern Canada. A review of conference origins may help to explain the significance of this union.

The Mennonite Conference of Ontario and Quebec had its roots in the first migration of Mennonites to Canada in 1786, with settlers coming from Switzerland and South Germany via Pennsylvania. Out of this group came the first Mennonite congregation in this country, The First Mennonite Church (1801), located in Vineland, Ontario. Ministers began meeting annually about 1810, laying the foundation for a conference. Conflicts over modernization and change led to a division in 1889; those who chose to remain with traditional worship and lifestyle became known as the Old Order Mennonite Church. In 1909, members who had moved to Saskatchewan and Alberta formed their own church body (see Northwest Mennonite Conference). Outreach in Quebec began in 1956, resulting in several new congregations.

The Western Ontario Mennonite Conference had its roots in the Amish migration from Europe to Ontario beginning in 1822. In the 1880s, the Amish divided into "House" and "Church" Amish—the house group became the Old Order Amish and the church group organized in 1923 as the Ontario Amish Mennonite Conference. This conference sent out the first Canadian Mennonite missionaries, to Argentina, in the early 1920s. The "Amish" name was dropped in the 1960s.

The Conference of United Mennonite Churches, the third partner in the Mennonite Conference of Eastern Canada, was established by immigrants from Russia who arrived in Ontario in the 1920s. This group was a provincial body of the Conference of Mennonites in Canada, founded in 1903 by Russian Mennonites in western Canada.

The story of the Conference of Mennonites in Canada begins in Manitoba and Saskatchewan. The first Mennonites from Russia, including the whole colony of Bergthal, arrived in Manitoba between 1874 and 1876. In the 1890s, immigrants from Russia, Prussia, and the United States settled in Saskatchewan. The Manitoba group formed the *Bergthaler Gemeinde* (church). The Saskatchewan group formed the *Rosenorter Gemeinde*. Leaders from these two groups expressed the desire to work together, and at a 1902 meeting hosted by Bishop Peter Regier of the Rosenorter church, a group of men laid the groundwork for the Conference of Mennonites in Central Canada (*Konferenz der Mennoniten im mittleren Kanada*). The first session of the new conference was held in Hochstadt, Manitoba (near Altona), in 1903.

A new wave of immigrants from Russia began arriving in 1924, greatly expanding the scope of this conference. New congregations from Ontario to British Columbia joined, and in 1932 the name was changed to General Conference of Mennonites in Canada. Provincial bodies were established in British Columbia, Alberta, Saskatchewan, Manitoba, and Ontario.

More Russian Mennonites arrived after World War II, both from Europe and via South America. With a major reorganization in 1959, the name was changed to Conference of Mennonites in Canada. From the beginning, most of its congregations were linked to the North American body, the General Conference Mennonite Church.

Recognizing the need for theological education, the conference established the Canadian Mennonite Bible College in Winnipeg in 1947. The college became part of Canadian Mennonite University in 1999.

The union of the Ontario conference with its two counterparts of Swiss and Amish background in 1988 led the way to the formation of Mennonite Church Canada in 1999. Today this national church body includes members from many cultures and parts of the globe, including indigenous people of Canada. Ministry to immigrants in recent decades has resulted in about 25

Steinmann Mennonite Church in Baden, Ontario, a congregation with Amish origins, is now part of Mennonite Church Canada.

Mennonite young people in Winnipeg protesting militarism.

congregations of various languages, including Chinese, Laotian, Vietnamese, Hispanic, Hmong, and Korean.

Mennonite Church Canada participates in inter-Mennonite organizations such as Mennonite Central Committee and the Council for International Ministries. It is a sponsor of Christian Peacemaker Teams, an ecumenical organization that places workers in areas of conflict. It is a member of both the Evangelical Fellowship of Canada and the Canadian Council of Churches, and is active in the Mennonite World Conference.

Distinctives

The theological foundation of Mennonite Church Canada is outlined in the *Confession of Faith in a Mennonite Perspective* (1995). The church's vision statement says, "God calls us to be followers of Jesus Christ and, by the power of the Holy Spirit, to grow as communities of grace, joy, and peace so that God's healing and hope flow through us to the world." The church seeks "to engage the world with the reconciling Gospel of Jesus Christ," according to the statement of purpose.

Mennonite Church Canada is organized through a General Board and three councils: Christian Witness (national and international ministries), Formation (education, leadership, and resources), and Support Services (communications and administration). Related to this structure is Canadian Women in Mission, organized both nationally and provincially. National programs include Native Ministry and Multicultural Ministry. International ministries include work in about 35 countries. The Witness Council works with Mennonite Church USA's Mission Network in several countries.

Made up of five area churches, Mennonite Church Canada polity is a blend of congregationalism and conference decision-making, with both congregations and area churches choosing delegates for the annual assembly. The budget of Mennonite Church Canada for 2006 was four million dollars.

Mennonite Church Canada is a partner with Mennonite Church USA in operating Associated Mennonite Biblical Seminary in Elkhart, Indiana, and in the Mennonite Publishing Network, which provides Sunday school curriculum and resources for congregations.

The campus of Canadian Mennonite University, founded in 1999 by the merger of three Mennonite colleges in Winnipeg.

Canoeing at Camp Moose Lake in Manitoba.

Mennonite Church Canada Area Churches

The five regional bodies that make up Mennonite Church Canada have their beginnings in yearly meetings of ministers and deacons. As congregations multiplied, provincial conferences were organized to provide fellowship and enable churches to work together. With the birth of Mennonite Church Canada in 1999, the regional bodies renamed themselves "churches" instead of conferences. Area churches have their own annual assemblies and appoint delegates to the national assembly.

The area churches operate their own programs and institutions, and most relate to regional programs such as prison ministries, hospital and university chaplaincy, immigration services, and counselling programs. Regional church staff assist congregations in choosing pastors and provide resources for pastors and congregations in areas such as Christian education, youth and young adult ministry, and planting new churches. Regional women's groups relate to each other within the national Women in Mission organization. The area churches are partners, along with Mennonite Church Canada and the Canadian Mennonite Publishing Service, in publishing *Canadian Mennonite*, a magazine available to all members.

Mennonite Church Alberta

Founded: 1929
Head office: Calgary
Schools: Rosthern Junior College (in partnership with Mennonite Church Saskatchewan)
Camp: Camp Valaqua

Members   **1,948**
200 are not part of the national church

Congregations   **17**
1 is not part of the national church

Members	3,906

Congregations	33
1 dually affiliated with Mennonite Brethren conference	

Mennonite Church British Columbia

Founded: 1935

Head office: Abbotsford

Schools: Columbia Bible College (partner with British Columbia Conference of Mennonite Brethren Churches)

Relates to Mennonite Educational Institute through supporting congregations

Camp: Camp Squeah

Members	13,905

Congregations	92
Mainly in Ontario, with 3 in Quebec, 1 in New Brunswick	

Mennonite Church Eastern Canada

Union of three conferences founded in 1810, 1923, and 1945

Head office: Kitchener

Schools: Conrad Grebel University College and Toronto Mennonite Theological Centre

Relates to Rockway Mennonite Collegiate and United Mennonite Educational Institute

Institutions/Programs: Mennonite and Brethren in Christ Resource Centre

Camps: Relates to Silver Lake Mennonite Camp, Hidden Acres Mennonite Camp, Ontario Mennonite Music Camp, Fraser Lake Camp, and Glenbrook Day Camp

Programs: Supports service ministries in Toronto (Jane Finch, Mennonite New Life Centre, Warden Woods), London (chaplaincy), Hamilton (Welcome Inn), Montreal (House of Friendship), and Kitchener (Mennonite Coalition for Refugee Support)

Members	10,282
Plus 2 native congregations	

Congregations	49
1 dually affiliated with Mennonite Brethren conference	

Mennonite Church Manitoba

Founded: 1947

Head office: Winnipeg

Schools: Relates to Westgate Mennonite Collegiate and Mennonite Collegiate Institute

Supports Winnipeg Centre for Ministry Studies (a partnership of 4 schools and 5 Manitoba Mennonite conferences)

Camps: Camps Assiniboia, Koinonia, and Moose Lake

Programs: Faith and Life Choirs, Recording studio

Mennonite Church Saskatchewan

Members	3,623
Congregations	34

Founded: 1959

Head office: Saskatoon

Schools: Rosthern Junior College (in partnership with Mennonite Church Alberta)

Camps: Camp Elim, Shekinah Retreat Centre, Youth Farm Bible Camp

Two young Mennonites examine an exhibit at a Mennonite Central Committee meeting. The one at the right is wearing a Remembrance Day pin made popular by MCC Ontario: "To remember is to work for peace."

Steinbach Bible College in Manitoba, founded in 1936, is operated by three Manitoba Mennonite conferences.

Evangelical Mennonite Conference

Members	**7,341**
Congregations	**59**

Location
Manitoba: 5,349 members in
  36 congregations
Alberta: 888 in 9 congregations
Ontario: 566 in 6 congregations
Saskatchewan: 357 in 6
  congregations
British Columbia: 181 in 2
  congregations

Head office
440 Main Street
Steinbach, MB R5G 1Z5

Schools
Steinbach Bible College
  (in partnership with Evangelical
  Mennonite Mission Conference
  and Choritzer Mennonite
  Conference)
Steinbach Christian High School
  (in partnership with Chortitzer
  Mennonite Conference and
  two evangelical congregations)
Winnipeg Centre for Ministry
  Studies (a partnership of 4
  schools and 5 Manitoba
  Mennonite conferences)

Periodicals
The Messenger
EMC Missionary Prayer Calendar
Theodidaktos (theology and
  education journal)

History

This conference has its beginnings in a revival movement in the Molotschna Mennonite Colony of southern Russia in 1812. In that year, a group of about 20 men, led by Klaas Reimer, left the established Mennonite church to form a new group, which became known as the *Kleine Gemeinde* (small church).

Reimer and his supporters objected to the way civil authority in the colony was replacing church discipline. They also called for more personal accountability and spiritual fervour in the church. The differences led to heated conflicts among church leaders, and government officials finally intervened to try to solve the conflict. With Reimer's ordination as bishop (*Aeltester*) in 1817, the painful split was finalized.

The Kleine Gemeinde was committed to a stricter discipline and separation from the world. The next years were a struggle for the fledgling group as it tried to curb excesses within the group and withstand persecution from the main church. The new church was finally recognized in 1843.

In 1874, most of the Kleine Gemeinde members in the Molotschna Colony joined the Bergthal Colony in the move to Manitoba. The reasons for emigration included the growing threats to the independence of Mennonite colonies: the Russian government had announced its intention to "Russianize" Mennonite schools and take away exemption to military service, originally promised in perpetuity.

45

A Bible study group from the Fish Creek Christian Fellowship, an Evangelical Mennonite Conference church in Calgary.

Some 60 Kleine Gemeinde families settled in the Steinbach and Morris areas of Manitoba; about 36 families went to Nebraska. (The U.S. Kleine Gemeinde group became part of the Evangelical Mennonite Brethren church in 1943.)

A renewal movement in 1881 split the Kleine Gemeinde church in Manitoba—about a third of the members left to join a group led by John Holdeman of Ohio. Holdeman emphasized new birth and spiritual zeal, along with nonconformity to the world. Popularly known as the Holdeman Church, this group's official name is Church of God in Christ, Mennonite. A rigid retrenching of the Kleine Gemeinde followed, leading to the exodus of more members. Many joined the Evangelical Mennonite Brethren Church (now called the Fellowship of Evangelical Bible Churches).

In 1948, about 100 Kleine Gemeinde families moved to Mexico, where they could live more separately and maintain control over their children's education. Ten years later, about half of these moved to Belize.

By 1950, Canadian congregations were functioning more autonomously, with self-appointed ministers. In 1952, the Kleine Gemeinde changed from a single church identity to a conference structure and adopted the name

Evangelical Mennonite Church. The name was changed to Evangelical Mennonite Conference (EMC) in 1959. Motivated by a spirit of mission and a need for farmland, some EMC families undertook "mission by colonization," moving to other areas of Manitoba and beyond and beginning new churches there. Congregations sprang up in Saskatchewan, northern British Columbia, and in Alberta's Peace River district.

Between 1946 and 1961, individual EMC members and churches were involved in the Western Gospel Mission, a venture in western Canada from which the conference gained some congregations. The first "foreign mission" worker was Suzanne Plett, sent by her congregation to Brazil in 1945. The conference's mission board began in 1953. It currently has mission workers in about two dozen countries.

While higher education was not encouraged until recent decades, the EMC did become a partner in the Steinbach Bible Academy, which began in the 1930s. Today, Steinbach Bible College is operated in partnership with the Evangelical Mennonite Mission Conference and the Chortitzer Mennonite Conference. The college shares its campus with the Steinbach Christian High School, founded in the 1940s.

The Kleine Gemeinde in Mexico and South America have retained the German name. In recent decades, some families have returned to Canada from Mexico, Belize, and Bolivia (see Kleine Gemeinde). These communities are not part of the Evangelical Mennonite Conference.

Distinctives

The Evangelical Mennonite Conference claims its roots in both the Radical Reformation and in evangelical Protestantism. "As Evangelical, we hold to scripture as our final authority in faith and practice, to a belief in Christ's finished work on the cross for our reconciliation, and to a life of discipleship based on the life of Christ and the teaching of scripture. As Mennonite, we are committed to following Christ daily in life; to baptism upon confession of faith and in living out our faith together as a church family; to expressing social concern, partly through a commitment to nonviolence; and by wider mission," states the introduction on the EMC website.

About 75 percent of the conference budget goes toward mission work in Canada and other countries. While the group's Low German ethnic roots remain visible, membership is increasingly diverse and leaders come from a variety of backgrounds. Women serve in leadership roles (some congregations have women pastors), but the conference does not ordain women to pastoral leadership.

One Quilt, Many Pieces

Recent decades have seen a renewed interest in the church's Anabaptist roots. With that has come the desire to train pastors in an Anabaptist context. The EMC was a partner in founding the Evangelical Anabaptist Seminary Program in 2002, now known as the Winnipeg Centre for Ministry Studies. The conference cooperates with other Mennonite groups in service, mission, and education programs, including the Inter-Mennonite Chaplaincy at the University of Manitoba. The EMC belongs to the Mennonite World Conference, Mennonite Central Committee, and the Council of Anabaptist International Ministries, as well as the Evangelical Fellowship of Canada and the Canadian Council of Christian Charities.

A student from Steinbach Bible College makes friends with First Nations children in the northern Manitoba community of Garden Hill during a school mission trip there. Steinbach Bible College is supported by the Evangelical Mennonite Conference.

Evangelical Mennonite Mission Conference

Members	**4,294**

Congregations	**29**

Location
Manitoba: 2,948 members in
16 congregations
Ontario: 957 in 6 congregations
Saskatchewan: 374 in 6
congregations
Alberta: 15 in 1 congregation

Head office
Box 52059
Niakwa P.O.
Winnipeg, MB R2M 5P9

Schools
Bethany College, Hepburn,
Saskatchewan (in partnership
with Saskatchewan and Alberta
Mennonite Brethren churches)
Steinbach Bible College, Steinbach,
Manitoba (in partnership with
Evangelical Mennonite
Conference and Chortitzer
Mennonite Conference)
Winnipeg Centre for Ministry
Studies (a partnership of 4
schools and 5 Manitoba
Mennonite conferences)

Programs
Gospel Message Ministries
(in partnership with Sommerfelder and Bergthaler churches)

Periodicals
The EMMC Recorder

History

The Evangelical Mennonite Confer-
ence has its roots in the Bergthal Colony migration from Russia to Manitoba in the 1870s.
Bergthal Mennonites settled on two reserves in
southern Manitoba, on the west and east sides
of the Red River. In the 1890s, a conservative
movement emerged out of the Bergthal church
on the West Reserve, leading to the formation
of the Sommerfelder Mennonite Church. In the
1930s, a revival movement swept through the
Sommerfelder church, dividing that group.

In 1937, four young ministers left the
Sommerfelder church to form a new church,
which met in the village of Rudnerweide.
Hence the new group of congregations was
organized as the *Rudnerweider Mennoniten
Gemeinde* (Rudnerweide Mennonite Church).
In 1939, the new group had just over 1,100
members.

Under its first bishop, William H. Falk, the
Rudnerweider church emphasized personal
conversion, Sunday school for children, youth
programs, and missions. The revival spread to
Saskatchewan, where several congregations
were established. The first missionary, John
Schellenberg, was sent out in the early 1940s.
The church sponsored a large slate of mission
workers, who served with various mission
organizations.

In 1959, the Rudnerweider church was
reorganized as the Evangelical Mennonite
Mission Conference (EMMC). This new

structure allowed for more autonomy and local development of congregations, while retaining joint ministries and annual gatherings. While the
conference was experiencing increased urbanization and a shift to English,
it was at the same time expanding its work among conservative, Low
German-speaking Mennonites in Canada and Latin America.

In 1957, the conference began a German-language radio ministry,
which has continued to this day. In 1963, *The Gospel Message* program
switched to Low German, produced by John D. Friesen in Saskatoon. This
program reaches Low German-speaking Mennonites across Canada, the
United States, Mexico, Belize, Bolivia, and Paraguay; CD distribution also
includes Germany and Russia. Since 1997, Gospel Message Ministries has
been a partnership of EMMC, the Sommerfelder Mennonite Church of
Manitoba, and the Bergthaler Mennonite Church of Saskatchewan.

In the 1960s, the EMMC inherited three mission stations when the
Western Gospel Mission dissolved, two in Manitoba and one in Saskatchewan. In the mid-1960s, the EMMC began mission work in Ontario
among Old Colony Mennonites returning to Canada from Mexico. This
led to a number of new congregations in Ontario and to the establishment
of the Aylmer Bible School to serve Low German-speaking Mennonites

A neighbourhood party at the North End Community Church in Winnipeg. This church
plant, which is attracting aboriginal young people, is a partnership of the EMMC, EMC and
Chortitzer conferences, along with Inner City Youth Alive.

from Mexico. The school disbanded in 2000.

During the 1960s, the conference also began mission work in Belize and Bolivia. More recently, the EMMC has worked with Low German-speaking Mennonites in Mexico, as well as Texas, Kansas, and Iowa, establishing about 25 mission congregations.

Distinctives

The Evangelical Mennonite Mission Conference is characterized by an emphasis on evangelism and missions. Strongly influenced by revivalism, the conference has also maintained its Mennonite identity. While women serve in a broad variety of ministry roles, the conference does not ordain women as pastors. Only those churches with members of Old Colony Mennonite background use German in their services.

Worshippers offer praise at the 2007 EMMC convention at Bethany College in Hepburn, Saskatchewan.

Recent decades have seen increasing cooperation with the Evangelical Mennonite Conference and the Mennonite Brethren. In Manitoba, the EMMC is a partner in operating Steinbach Bible College and in the Winnipeg Centre for Ministry Studies (established in 2002). It also cooperates in the Inter-Mennonite Chaplaincy at the University of Manitoba. In Saskatchewan, the EMMC became a co-sponsor of Bethany College in 1995.

The EMMC participates in inter-Mennonite organizations such as Mennonite Central Committee, Mennonite Foundation of Canada, and Mennonite World Conference. The conference is also a member of the Evangelical Fellowship of Canada.

2
Regional Conferences

This trainload of Canadian wheat headed for Iran was collected by the Canadian Foodgrains Bank, an interdenominational coalition that includes Mennonite Central Committee.

The two church bodies in this section have very different stories. The Chortitzer Mennonite Conference was formed in Manitoba in the 1870s by immigrants from Russia and still retains traces of its rural, Low German heritage. Most of its congregations are in Manitoba.

The Northwest Mennonite Conference, based in Alberta, has a mixed parentage of Swiss Mennonite homesteaders from Ontario and immigrants from the United States. Conservative dress and lifestyle are disappearing as the conference focuses on evangelism and church planting. Part of the Mennonite Church (North American body) before it integrated with the General Conference Mennonite Church in 2002, the Northwest Conference is now pursuing an independent course.

Both the Chortitzer and Northwest conferences remain in touch with other Mennonites through organizations such as Mennonite Central Committee and the Mennonite Foundation of Canada.

There is one congregation in northern Ontario that relates only to groups in the United States. The Morson Community Bible Fellowship, begun in 1961 as a mission outreach by Mennonites from Iowa and Indiana, has 27 members, both native and non-native. It relates to Mennonite Church USA and to the Anabaptist Native Fellowship of Churches facilitated by Eastern Mennonite Missions in Pennsylvania.

Grunthal Chortitzer Mennonite Church in Manitoba staged its own "American Idol" show recently under the theme "So you think you can serve!" Shown here are the judges.

Chortitzer Mennonite Conference

Members	1,700

Congregations	13

Location
10 congregations in Manitoba, 1 in Saskatchewan, 2 in British Columbia

Head office
Box 968
Steinbach, MB R5G 1M7

Schools
Steinbach Bible College (in partnership with Evangelical Mennonite Conference and Evangelical Mennonite Mission Conference)
Steinbach Christian High School (in partnership with Evangelical Mennonite Conference and two evangelical congregations)
Winnipeg Centre for Ministry Studies (a partnership of 4 schools and 5 Manitoba conferences)

Periodicals
The Chronicle

History

This conference has its roots in the Bergthal Colony of South Russia. When the whole Bergthal Colony moved to Manitoba between 1874 and 1876, members settled on two "reserves" in southern Manitoba, one on each side of the Red River. This conference grew out of the churches established in the East Reserve, today the area around Steinbach.

Bishop Gerhard Wiebe, who resided in the East Reserve, presided over both reserves until 1882. In that year, Johann Funk was ordained bishop of the Bergthaler churches in the West Reserve (area around Altona). There dissension was growing over public education, participation in municipal politics, and other issues, and Funk sided with those who favoured change. The majority of the church in the West Reserve rejected Funk's leadership, and in 1894 Abraham Doerksen from the village of Sommerfeld was ordained to serve those who opposed Funk. Doerksen's group took the name Sommerfelder Mennonite Church.

The Bergthaler settlers in the East Reserve took the name Mennonite Church of Chortitz (the resident village of their bishop). Funk's followers retained the name Bergthaler Mennonite Church; this group was a founding member of what became Mennonite Church Canada. (The current Bergthaler Church of Saskatchewan developed independently and is not connected to the Manitoba churches.)

The Chortitzer churches, like the Sommer-

Ministers and deacon couples from the Chortitzer Mennonite Conference enjoy curling at a retreat in Manitoba.

felder, maintained conservative ways, resisting innovations such as harmony singing, Sunday schools, or youth gatherings. Authority resided in the bishop and the ministers. Worship was in High German and Low German, the latter the language of everyday life. The Chortitzer and Sommerfelder churches maintained ties until about 1958.

The Chortitzer church has remained a fairly small, cohesive group. In 1948, about 1,700 of the most conservative members left for Paraguay, opening the doors to change in the Canadian church. In the 1960s and 70s, English was gradually adopted and the group moved to a conference structure. Christian education became important, with congregations beginning Sunday schools, young people's programs, and Bible study meetings.

The late 1950s saw a new interest in missions and outreach. Today numerous members are serving under the Chortitzer mission program or with other mission organizations.

In 1995, Zion Mennonite Church, a congregation in the West Reserve, joined the Chortitzer conference. Zion was formed in 1980 by a breakaway group from the Old Colony Mennonite Church. The congregation became established with the help of Chortitzer conference leaders, introducing Sunday school and a youth organization.

Distinctives

The Chortitzer Conference, with the Sommerfelder Mennonite Church, is the conservative wing of the Bergthaler immigration to Manitoba. The Chortitzer conference is still a cohesive group, but it is becoming more diverse as each congregation develops its own character. Today, one congregation uses only the German language for worship, three use both German and English, and the remaining have services only in English. A number of congregations have paid pastors, but smaller churches have lay leaders. In 2002, the conference dissolved the *Waisenamt* (literally, orphan agency), a church trust fund that had begun in Russia.

Congregations are served by one bishop who is part of an executive committee that heads the conference. The conference sponsors a Low

German radio broadcast, *Dee Harrliche Botschaft* (The Holy Gospel), which reaches Mennonites in Manitoba, Paraguay, Bolivia, and Mexico. There has been a shift toward higher education. The Chortitzer conference is a partner in operating Steinbach Bible College, together with the Evangelical Mennonite Conference and the Evangelical Mennonite Mission Conference. It is one of five partners in the Winnipeg Centre for Ministry Studies.

The Chortitzer conference also cooperates in inter-Mennonite organizations such as Mennonite Central Committee and Mennonite Foundation of Canada.

A baptismal class with pastors Bill Janzen and John Unger at Osler Mission Chapel in Saskatchewan.

The West Zion Mennonite Church in Carstairs, Alberta, established in 1901, was the first congregation in what became the Northwest Mennonite Conference.

An ordination prayer for Pastor Trevor Kiriaka and his wife Phyllis at West Zion Mennonite Church in Alberta in June 2007. Officiating is Mal Braun, Northwest conference minister.

Northwest Mennonite Conference

Members	1,100
Congregations	14

Location
Alberta

Head office
2025-20th Street
Didsbury, AB T0M 0W0

Periodicals
Points of Connection newsletter

History

As early as the 1890s, Swiss Mennonites from Ontario and the United States began moving to Alberta to homestead. Ontario Mennonites settled in the Carstairs-Didsbury and High River areas. Families from Pennsylvania settled near Mayton and Duchess, and a group from Nebraska with Amish Mennonite roots established the Salem Mennonite Church near Tofield in 1910.

In 1903, the Ontario Mennonite Conference commissioned Ontario leader S. F. Coffman to visit the Alberta settlements, ordain pastors, and help organize churches. The Alberta District Conference was formed in 1904 as an affiliate of the Ontario conference, with Amos S. Bauman of Mayton chosen by lot as the first bishop. (Bauman, who held controversial views such as "the second work of grace," or perfectionism, was removed from his position in 1906 by Ontario leaders.)

In 1905 and 1906, a number of Swiss Mennonite families from Ontario moved to Guernsey, Saskatchewan, and established a congregation there. They affiliated with the Alberta conference, so in 1907 the conference was renamed the Alberta-Saskatchewan Mennonite Conference. Eli S. Hallman, who led the Guernsey church, was ordained bishop of the new conference, which soon became independent of the Ontario body.

In the late 1940s, the conference began mission posts in Smith, Bluesky, and Eaglesham,

Alberta; the first two are still member congregations. In 1949, a small Hutterite group near Stirling joined the conference. The years 1955 to 1973 were characterized by voluntary service projects in northern areas, with workers coming from the United States. Many of these volunteers remained in Canada after their terms were over. In later years, congregations were established in Edmonton and Calgary, including several Hispanic churches. The conference also had congregations in Montana and Alaska for a time. The Guernsey congregation closed its doors in 2006.

As a district conference of the North American denomination called the Mennonite Church, the Alberta conference changed its name to Northwest Conference of the Mennonite Church in 1972. In 1993, it became the Northwest Mennonite Conference. (The Northwest Conference and the Mennonite Conference of Ontario made up about 10 percent of the North American denomination.) With the integration of the Mennonite Church and the General Conference Mennonite Church, and the separation into Mennonite Church USA and Canada in 1999, the Northwest Conference lost its structural connection to the Mennonite Church. It became an associate member of Mennonite Church Canada for a time but decided in 2003 to discontinue this relationship. The Northwest Conference is now independent.

Distinctives

This conference inherited the blend of conservative Mennonitism and evangelicalism that characterized its Swiss Mennonite parents. In the early days, conservative dress and head coverings for women went hand-in-hand with a passion for outreach and church planting. Today the conference is a blend of rural and urban, Anglo and Hispanic congregations, and one Chinese church in Edmonton, which is also affiliated with Mennonite Church Alberta. A special Macedonia budget provides funds for church planting and other mission projects. The conference is governed by a six-member board.

Recent years have seen the loss of about seven congregations because of closings and other factors. For example, its former U.S. congregations now relate to Mennonite Church USA, and Holyrood Mennonite Church in Edmonton joined Mennonite Church Canada.

The Northwest Conference continues to relate to inter-Mennonite organizations such as Mennonite Central Committee and Mennonite Foundation of Canada.

3
Conservative Churches of Russian-German Origin

Maria Dyck and Hein Rempel manage CHPD in Aylmer, Ontario, the only Low German radio station in Canada. *De Brigj* (The Bridge) provides news, music and announcements for Mennonites from Mexico who have moved to Ontario. The station received a government grant of $110,000 in 2006 to develop public education broadcasts. The Chortitzer and Evangelical Mennonite Mission conferences in Manitoba also sponsor some Low German broadcasts.

The groups in this section are called *conservative* churches because they have sought to maintain traditional worship patterns and ways of life. Many members live close to each other in small communities, speaking Low German brought from Russia in the 1870s. In some cases, Low German has replaced High German as the language of worship as well. Recent decades have seen more English in church, especially in the Sommerfelder group.

Each group is led by a bishop who supervises the lay ministers elected by the congregation. Ministers receive no remuneration. Higher education is suspect, by and large. Most of these groups participate to some extent in inter-Mennonite organizations such as Mennonite Central Committee, and the Ontario groups use the Mennonite Savings and Credit Union.

Dress and other customs vary. In the Old Colony, Reinland, and Church of God in Christ, Mennonite (Holdeman), women wear black head coverings or kerchiefs and men dark clothes. The Sommerfelder group is the least conservative, with Sunday schools, musical instruments, and English hymnals. It is the group most involved in inter-Mennonite activities. The Church of God in Christ, Mennonite (Holdeman), is the most self-sufficient and insular, and is known for its strict church discipline. The Old Colony is a loosely connected group of churches that has some contact across provincial borders but no formal organization.

In addition to the groups listed here, there are a number of independent congregations that are difficult to categorize. One example is the Rosenberg Mennonite Church in Arborg, Manitoba, an offshoot of the Kleine Gemeinde church, with 150 members. For the purposes of this book, it is estimated that there are about 12 such independent churches with about 1,000 members.

Bergthaler Mennonite Church of Saskatchewan

Members	846
Congregations	6

Location
Saskatchewan, 1 in Ontario

Schools
Valley Christian Academy in Osler, K-12

Institutions/Programs
Home for Seniors in Warman (owned jointly with Old Colony Mennonites)

History

This group has its origins in the migration of the Bergthal Mennonite Colony from Russia to Manitoba in the 1870s. Mennonites in Manitoba were given two reserves, one on each side of the Red River. In the early 1890s, some of the settlers in the West Reserve began moving to Saskatchewan, where two new Mennonite reserves had opened up: Rosthern in 1893 and Swift Current in 1900. Reasons for the move included more available land and the threat of an English school system in Manitoba. Some members of another Manitoba group, the Old Colony Mennonite Church, moved to Saskatchewan for the same reasons.

Meanwhile, the Bergthaler Mennonite Church in Manitoba divided in 1894 over higher education and other issues. The minority, which favoured education and other changes, retained the Bergthaler name. The conservative majority in the West Reserve took the name Sommerfelder Mennonite Church, while Bergthalers in the East Reserve changed their name to Chortitzer Mennonite Church. The Saskatchewan group's loyalties were with the conservative groups, but it retained the Bergthaler name. The Bergthaler Mennonite Church of Manitoba dissolved as an organization in 1972; its congregations are now members of Mennonite Church Canada.

Bishop David Stoesz of the Chortitzer church came to Saskatchewan in 1893 to organize the Bergthaler church there. The Saskatchewan church also absorbed later settlers who moved to this province from Russia and from the United States.

A dispute over leadership led to the dissolution of the Rosthern congregation in 1896, and the group divided in 1908 over wedding rituals. Bishop Kornelius Epp left in 1908 to form his own church and led some members to Mexico in the 1920s. The next bishop, Aaron Zacharias, led a group to Paraguay in 1926. Both these groups left Canada because the government refused to allow them to operate their own schools.

The group remaining in Saskatchewan was reunited under Bishop Cornelius Hamm. The *Waisenamt* (church trust fund) fell apart during the Great Depression of the 1930s. Many impoverished Bergthalers resettled in northern Saskatchewan. A Sunday school program began in the 1940s, and worship shifted from High German to Low German, the language of everyday life.

Since the 1940s there have been several migrations of Saskatchewan Bergthalers: to Paraguay in 1948, to Honduras in 1951 (this group was refused entry and had to return home), and to Bolivia in 1962. The moves represented the group's desire to resist conformity to the world and to maintain tradition. In 1979 and 1983 the group experienced further divisions over use of English and accommodation to culture.

The Saskatchewan Bergthaler maintained contact with Manitoba Sommerfelder and Chortitzer Mennonite churches until about 1958. In that year, the Swift Current congregation divided, with half the group joining the Evangelical Mennonite Mission Conference. Today the Bergthaler church has six congregations, including one that was formed in Ontario in 2001.

Distinctives

Members of this group are primarily farmers, living simple, modest lives separate from the surrounding culture. They are similar in many ways to Old Colony Mennonites; the two groups share a home for seniors in Warman. The Saskatchewan Bergthaler have no formal organization. Ministers are unpaid and elected from within the congregation. Worship is in English, with musical instruments to accompany singing.

Since 1984, the Bergthaler church has participated in Mennonite Central Committee. Some congregations use the financial services of Mennonite Foundation of Canada and Mennonite Mutual Insurance (Alberta) Ltd.

Other Bergthaler Churches

Besides the congregations belonging to the Bergthaler Mennonite Church of Saskatchewan, there are independent Bergthaler congregations in Saskatchewan, Alberta, and Ontario. For example, four congregations in northern Alberta call themselves Evangelical Church (Bergthaler Mennonite). A congregation called the Old Bergthaler Mennonite Church, located near Hague, Saskatchewan, relates to the Reinland Mennonite Church in Manitoba.

In addition, seven congregations within Mennonite Church Canada—six in Manitoba and one in Alberta—have retained their Bergthaler name, reflecting their origins in the Bergthaler Mennonite Church in Manitoba, which dissolved in 1972.

The plain, functional style of this church in Saskatchewan is typical of the Saskatchewan Bergthaler and other conservative groups.

Hungry bikers fill their plates after a "Bike the Whiteshell" fundraiser for Mennonite Central Committee in Manitoba.

Sommerfelder Mennonite Church of Manitoba

Members	5,014

Congregations	13

Location
Southern Manitoba

Schools
Mennonite Collegiate Institute (board membership and financial support)
Relates to 6 inter-Mennonite schools (grades 1-12)

Institutions/Programs
Board membership in various Mennonite institutions

History

This church grew out of the Bergthal Mennonite settlement in Manitoba. When the Bergthal Colony moved to Canada from Russia between 1874 and 1876, families settled on two "reserves" in southern Manitoba, one on each side of the Red River. Bishop Gerhard Wiebe presided over the church in both reserves during the first years of settlement.

Church life was conservative—there were no Sunday schools or youth gatherings, and singing was strictly unison. Authority resided in the bishop (Aeltester) and the lay ministers. Worship was in German, with Low German as the language of everyday life.

In 1882, Johann Funk was ordained bishop of the church in the West Reserve (Altona area). Here dissension was growing over public education, participation in municipal politics, mission outreach, and other issues. Funk headed a minority group that favoured teacher training, fellowship with other believers, and other progressive innovations. The majority of the church rejected Funk's leadership.

In 1894, Abraham Doerksen from the village of Sommerfeld was ordained to serve those who opposed Funk. Doerksen's group took the name Sommerfelder Mennonite Church, after the village in which Doerksen resided. Funk's minority group retained the name Bergthaler Mennonite Church.

The Sommerfelder church maintained a

relationship with the Bergthal settlers of the East Reserve (Steinbach area), who had taken the name Chortitzer Mennonite Church, and with Bergthal members in Saskatchewan. (Some Bergthal families from Manitoba had moved to Saskatchewan in the 1890s, where they formed the Bergthaler Mennonite Church of Saskatchewan.) Cooperation also continued with the Bergthaler church from which it had divided. The *Waisenamt* (church trust fund) was not divided until 1907, when the Bergthaler wanted to incorporate it legally. In many villages the two groups continued to operate elementary schools together. During both world wars, the Sommerfelder cooperated with other Mennonite groups in representations to Ottawa to establish alternatives to military service.

More conservative Sommerfelders continued to be restless under the threat of an English school system, believing this would endanger their separatist way of life. In 1922, a number of Sommerfelder families left for Mexico, along with Old Colony and Saskatchewan Bergthaler members, some 6,000 people in all. There they set up colonies, with schools regulated by church leaders. Some of these later moved on to Bolivia, where they were even more isolated from the surrounding culture. Beginning in 1928, about 7,800 people from the Sommerfelder, Chortitzer, and Saskatchewan Bergthaler churches left for Paraguay, where they established the Menno Colony. In 1948, a second migration to Mexico and Paraguay occurred from among the Manitoba Sommerfelder and Chortitzer groups.

Some of these families later returned to Canada. The Manitoba conference maintains some contact with the Sommerfelder Colony in Paraguay, which has five congregations.

The Sommerfeld group in Manitoba suffered two major schisms. In 1937, a renewal movement resulted in a new conference, the Rudnerweide Mennonite Church (now Evangelical Mennonite Mission Conference). In 1958, a conservative faction led by 12 of the 16 ministers withdrew, ostensibly because they opposed electricity in the church buildings. These ministers formed the Reinland Mennonite Church.

In recent years, the conference has established a congregation in Seminole, Texas, among Mennonites returning from Mexico. It is served by the Manitoba bishop.

Distinctives

While the Sommerfelder church has remained fairly conservative in its church life, changes have been rapid since the 1970s. Sunday school had begun in the 1950s, and the 1970s and 80s brought young people's meetings, English hymnals, an easing of restrictions on dress (plain, black clothes were no longer legislated for worship and weddings), and other innovations. One bishop serves the whole church, elected for life. Ministers are also elected for life and serve without remuneration. Each minister serves the entire church, preaching in different congregations according to a set rotation. Ministers still wear darks suits and shirts, with no ties.

The Sommerfelder church has board representation in Mennonite organizations such as Mennonite Central Committee Canada and Eden Health Care Services, as well as homes for seniors in Altona and Winkler. Individual families relate

The windmill at the Mennonite Heritage Village in Steinbach, Manitoba, is a replica of historic windmills built by Mennonites in the Netherlands.

to six schools that serve conservative Mennonites in Manitoba (Winkler, Steinbach, and Austin areas).

Independent Sommerfelder Churches

In addition to the Manitoba conference, there are at least 6 independent Sommerfelder congregations: 1 in Vanderhoof, British Columbia; 1 in La Crete, and 1 in Tabor, Alberta; 1 in Swift Current, Saskatchewan; 2 near Aylmer, Ontario.

The traditional house-barn dwelling, brought from Europe, can still be seen in Russian Mennonite villages on the prairies.

Reinland Mennonite Church

Members	3,000
Congregations	7

Location
Manitoba: 5 congregations
Alberta: 2 (plus 1 independent)

History

In 1958, a division occurred in the Sommerfelder Mennonite Church in Manitoba, a church that had been formed in the 1890s by settlers from the Bergthal Colony in Russia. The immediate reason for the division was the introduction of electricity into Sommerfelder church buildings. Many saw this as confirmation that the church was accommodating itself to the world and losing its distinctives.

About 800 members (a fifth of the membership), along with 12 of the 16 ministers, left the Sommerfelder church and formed the Reinland Mennonite Church (*Reinländer Mennoniten Gemeinde*). Reinland was the name of the Manitoba municipality in which the Mennonites settled in the 1870s. (The original settlers came from both the Bergthal Colony and the "Old Colony" of Chortitza in Russia. The Old Colony group originally called its church the Reinland Mennonite Church, but later adopted the name Old Colony Mennonite Church. In recent years, breakaways from the Old Colony church in Ontario have reclaimed the Reinland name. See Old Colony Mennonite Churches.)

The Reinland church was concerned to maintain old worship patterns, with unison singing, black dress for worship and weddings, and the German language (primarily Low German). This new group built even more plain, white church buildings, initially without electricity. Churches were built at Blumenfeld, Altona, Winkler, and Austin, Manitoba, in 1958. In 1960, some families of Chortitzer Mennonite origin formed a Reinland congregation at Grunthal, Manitoba. Mennonites returning from Mexico formed another at Rainy River, Ontario, in 1966.

In 1968, a number of families, led by their bishop, immigrated to Bolivia. Settlers from Saskatchewan and Paraguay joined them to establish a Reinlander congregation there. In 1979, another church was founded at the Swift Current Colony in Mexico; it grew to over 3,000 members in five locations. Other groups were organized at Santa Rita, Mexico, and Seminole, Texas, by Mennonites who had moved there from Mexico.

In recent years, some of the Reinland members from Bolivia have returned to Canada, settling in northern Alberta (Vauxhall and Worsley). These two congregations are served by the bishop of the Reinland Mennonite Church in Manitoba, William Friesen. The Manitoba church also relates to an independent Reinland congregation near La Crete, Alberta. Friesen also ordained the ministers and bishop of the Reinland Mennonite Fellowship Church near Aylmer, Ontario, which has three congregations.

The Reinland churches in Manitoba, Alberta, and Ontario meet as a conference every other year, joined by the Old Bergthaler Mennonite Church near Hague, Saskatchewan.

The oldest Mennonite church building in western Canada, built in 1876 and remodelled in the 1940s, located in the village of Reinland in Manitoba.

Distinctives

The Reinland Mennonite community is similar to the Old Colony Mennonite Church in terms of conservative lifestyle, dress, and separation from society. For church, women wear long, black dresses and black kerchiefs; men wear black pants and dark shirts without ties. Low German is the primary language of worship, but English is also used. There are no musical instruments in the church.

Most churches now have Sunday school and young people's groups, as well as weekly Bible studies. Church leadership consists of a bishop and lay, unpaid ministers who meet regularly to conduct church business. The bishop presides over baptisms, communion, selection of ministers and deacons, and ordinations. The church does not have its own institutions or periodical. Children attend public schools.

Related Reinland Groups

Friedensfelder Mennonite Church (*Friedensfelder Mennoniten Gemeinde*) was formed in 1986 in protest to electricity being installed in Reinland church buildings, a symbol of gradual accommodation to the world. This independent group has one congregation in Gnadenthal, Manitoba, with about 25 members. The church strives to maintain the conservative values that originally gave rise to the Reinland church.

For other related groups, see the Reinland Mennonite Fellowship Church under "Old Colony Mennonite Churches" and the Old Bergthaler Mennonite Church under "Bergthaler Mennonite Church of Saskatchewan."

This Old Colony Mennonite family left Mexico to make a new life in Alberta.

Old Colony Mennonite Churches

Members	9,044
Congregations	21

Location
Ontario: 4,493 members in 10 congregations
Alberta: 2,377 in 4 congregations
Manitoba: 1,110 in 5 congregations (includes German Old Colony with 310 members in 2 congregations)
British Columbia: 350 in 1 congregation
Saskatchewan: 264 in 1 congregation

Schools
Alberta: 4 elementary schools
Manitoba: relate to 3 inter-Mennonite schools (grades 1-12)
Ontario: 3 schools (grades 1-12)

History

The Old Colony or Fuerstenland Mennonites were part of the migration from Russia to Manitoba in the 1870s, along with the Bergthaler Mennonites. Both Fuerstenland and Bergthal were daughter colonies of the "Old Colony" of Chortitza, the first Mennonite colony established in Russia.

In Manitoba, true to the Mennonite custom of naming churches according to location, the Fuerstenland group called itself the Reinland Mennonite Church, after the municipality in which the church was located. Later it became known as the Old Colony Mennonite Church. (This group is not related to the current Reinland Mennonite Church of Manitoba.) In 1888, a number of Old Colony members were converted to a more evangelical faith by Mennonite Brethren mission workers from the United States, also recent immigrants from Russia. The converts established a church near Winkler, Manitoba, the first Mennonite Brethren congregation in Canada.

In 1895, motivated by the threat of English-language schools, some Old Colony families moved to the Rosthern area of Saskatchewan, where another reserve had been set aside for Mennonites. Another migration from Manitoba occurred in 1905 when a settlement was begun near Swift Current, Saskatchewan. In the 1920s, a substantial number of Old Colony Mennonites left

Manitoba for Mexico and Paraguay, where they could preserve their separate way of life.

In 1936, the Manitoba group officially organized as the Old Colony Mennonite Church. During the 1930s, a number of families from Saskatchewan moved to Alberta's Peace River area, and in the 1940s an Old Colony settlement was founded in northern British Columbia, near Prespatou. The one Saskatchewan congregation is located at Neuanlage, just north of Saskatoon.

A major development in the past few decades has been the return of thousands of Old Colony families from Mexico, settling mainly in Ontario, Manitoba, and Alberta. Those who settled in Ontario organized as a church in the 1960s, with the help of leaders from western Canada. The Ontario church is now the largest Old Colony group in Canada. (Aylmer, a centre of Old Colony settlement in Ontario, is the site of Canada's only Low German radio station, begun in 2003.)

In the 1980s, two new groups emerged out of the Old Colony church. In 1980, about 250 members left to form the Zion Mennonite Church in Manitoba. This congregation joined Chortitzer Mennonite Conference in 1995. In Ontario, a breakaway group formed in 1984, calling itself the New Reinland Church of Ontario. This latter group has since divided again (see Reinland churches below). In Manitoba, the German Old Colony Mennonite Church emerged in 2003, retaining all-German worship like its sister churches west of Manitoba. The two congregations in the German Old Colony church relate to the Old Colony churches in other provinces and in the United States.

Distinctives

Although practices vary, Old Colony members have resisted cultural assimilation and education and have remained separate from other Mennonite groups. They are the Russian Mennonite counterparts to Old Order groups in the Swiss Mennonite tradition. While Old Colony members in Mexico and Bolivia have resisted technology (some groups forbidding rubber tires for tractors), the church in Canada does not have restrictions against cars or other technology. (The most isolated group in Cecil Lake, British Columbia, which allowed no cars or government pensions, recently dissolved.)

Many of the women, particularly those who have returned from Mexico, are recognizable by their dark print dresses, severe hairstyles, and black kerchiefs. Members have retained the German language (primarily

Volunteer Susana Klassen who works at an MCC Thrift Store in Aylmer, Ontario, wears the black headscarf and conservative dress of Old Colony Mennonites returning from Mexico.

Low German) for worship, although some English is used. Hymn singing is unison, in a slow, chant-like style. Sermons, by lay ministers, are often read.

The Old Colony Mennonite Church is loosely organized, with many independent congregations. There is some fellowship between provincial groups. It is difficult to estimate membership because a considerable number of families move back and forth between Mexico and Canada for seasonal work. Many Old Colony Mennonites, while retaining traditional dress and customs, claim no church membership at all. Some Old Colony churches participate in Mennonite Central Committee and other church-related local organizations.

Other Old Colony Groups

New Reinland Mennonite Church of Ontario. In the early 1980s, the Old Colony Church in Ontario experienced considerable tensions over leadership, use of English, and programs for youth. Several dissenting ministers left in 1984 to form the New Reinland Mennonite Church of Ontario (no connection to the Reinland Mennonite Church in Manitoba). Led by a bishop, the group continues to follow traditional Old Colony practices, except for greater use of English in worship. It has its own burial society. The New Reinland Church has one congregation in Wheatley, Ontario, with 250 members.

Reinland Mennonite Fellowship Church. This group split off from the New Reinland Mennonite Church in 1994 in order to maintain more conservative ways. Worship and lifestyle are virtually the same as the Old Colony, but women do not wear distinctive clothing. Worship is in German, although exceptions are made for weddings and funerals. Ministers wear black. This group relates to the Reinland Mennonite Church in Manitoba, whose bishop ordained the Ontario leadership. The Ontario group is led by a bishop, five ministers, and a deacon. The Reinland Mennonite Fellowship has three congregations in the Aylmer area, with 975 members.

Kleine Gemeinde Mennonite Churches

Members	**726**
Congregations	**8**

Location

Ontario: 22 members in 4 congregations (southern Ontario)
Manitoba: 200 in 1 congregation (near Gimli)
Nova Scotia: 156 in 2 congregations
Alberta: 150 in 1 congregation (Grassy Lake)

Schools

6 schools (up to grade 12)

This group shares a history with the Evangelical Mennonite Conference. The *Kleine Gemeinde* (small church) began as a revival movement in Russia in 1812, and most of its members moved to Manitoba in the 1870s. In 1948, about 100 Kleine Gemeinde families moved to Mexico, where they could live more separately and maintain control over their children's education. Later, some of these moved to Belize and Bolivia.

While the Kleine Gemeinde in Canada reorganized as the Evangelical Mennonite Conference in 1959, these migrant groups who left Canada kept the German name. They are not affiliated with the Canadian conference.

In the early 1980s, some Kleine Gemeinde families began returning to Canada, and they have settled in four provinces. In Nova Scotia, they established Northfield colony in 1984, and another group settled in the Annapolis Valley in 2000. Some Northfield families moved to Ontario in the late 1990s to begin congregations in Leamington and Dresden.

In Ontario, where congregations have attracted many Old Colony Mennonites returning from Mexico, worship is entirely in the German language, although the church names are in English without a Kleine Gemeinde designation. The church in Leamington, for example, is called Cornerstone Community Church. The Manitoba congregation, called the InterLake Mennonite Fellowship, worships mainly in English.

Most congregations have their own schools, including high school. They use curriculum from Christian Light Publications based in Harrisonburg, Virginia. Ministers from across the country meet yearly, and Canadians meet with counterparts in Belize or Mexico every other year.

Church of God in Christ, Mennonite

Members	4,664
Congregations	52

Location

Alberta: 1,445 members in 14 congregations

British Columbia: 405 in 5 congregations

Manitoba: 1,842 in 17 congregations

New Brunswick: 57 in 1 congregation

Nova Scotia: 121 in 2 congregations

Ontario: 225 in 4 congregations

Quebec: 28 in 2 congregations

Saskatchewan: 541 in 7 congregations

Canadian office

Box 180, Rt. 1
Ste. Anne, MB R5H 1R1

Schools

Elementary schools in each congregation (up to grade 9)

Institutions/Programs

Christian Disaster Relief
Gospel Publishers
Gospel Tract and Bible Society
Mennonite Aid Union

Periodicals

Messenger of Truth

History

In terms of origin, this group could be listed under Swiss Conservative churches, but the Canadian branch took root in a Russian Mennonite community.

In 1859, a Swiss Mennonite from Ohio named John Holdeman left his Mennonite church to establish what he called "the true church which began with the Apostles" (see www.Holdeman.org). He was critical of the formalism and lack of spiritual vitality in the Mennonite church and advocated stricter separation from the world. His charismatic preaching and writings soon began to attract people to the new movement.

The Church of God in Christ, Mennonite, popularly known as the Holdeman church, exercised more rigorous church discipline and nonconformity, along with an emphasis on repentance and conversion. The movement attracted some followers among the Amish in Ontario; instead of organizing a congregation there, however, the Ontario followers moved to Michigan and joined the congregation there.

In 1881, Peter Toews, the bishop of the Kleine Gemeinde in Manitoba (now the Evangelical Mennonite Conference), invited Holdeman to come and preach in Manitoba. Attracted by Holdeman's synthesis of biblical ethics and assurance of salvation, Toews joined the Holdeman church, drawing one-third of the Kleine Gemeinde membership with him. Thus Holdeman's movement took root in Canada.

A Holdeman (Church of God in Christ, Mennonite) church building in Nova Scotia.

In 1902, several Holdeman families from Oregon (of Swiss Mennonite origin) moved to Linden, Alberta, where they were joined by their Russian Mennonite counterparts from Manitoba. Beginning in 1928, Holdeman Mennonites from Linden and Manitoba moved to the Peace River area in northern Alberta and established congregations there. In the 1940s and 1950s, families moved to British Columbia and Ontario as well. More recently, Holdeman communities have located in Saskatchewan and in Atlantic Canada.

Annual revival meetings began in the 1920s, mission work in the 1930s. The Canadian church has mission programs in five provinces as well as voluntary service units in Newfoundland and Quebec. Mission work is also carried out in Central and South America, India, Nigeria, the Philippines, and Europe. In 2005, the church had a worldwide membership of about 20,600, with 18,130 members in North America.

Publishing has been a high priority since the beginning (John Holdeman was a prolific writer in both German and English). Besides printing books and doctrinal material, the conference has a tract ministry, with the Canadian office in St. Anne, Manitoba. The church's periodical, *Messenger of Truth*, dates back to the early twentieth century.

Distinctives

One of the defining features of the Church of God in Christ, Mennonite, is its self-sufficiency and separation, not only from society but also from other Mennonite groups. The church emphasizes personal salvation in Christ and a holy life, separate from worldly pursuits. "A true Christian may not love the world nor conform to the ways of the world," says a church statement. "Therefore, fashion, pleasure and entertainment, professional sports, politics, prestigious business, idolatrous art, etc., are avoided (Luke 16:15; 1 Peter 4:1-4)."

The church has maintained a strict practice of church discipline, including excommunication and avoidance (shunning) of the excommunicated person. Leaving the Holdeman church is considered a mark of losing one's salvation. Members are to marry within the Holdeman church.

Nonresistance means no participation in civil or political affairs, including voting. Members do pay taxes and participate in the Canadian medical system. The church has its own mutual aid and disaster relief programs, as well as homes for seniors. Virtually every congregation operates its own elementary school, grades one through nine.

Modest clothing and lifestyle are emphasized: men have beards and women wear black head coverings over uncut hair. Worship takes place in plain buildings; singing is in four-part harmony with no musical instruments. Ministers and deacons are chosen from within the group by ballot. A General Conference, made up of ministers, deacons, and other delegates, meets every five to ten years for decision making.

In the United States, membership still reflects the church's beginnings among Mennonites of Swiss-German and Kansas-Prussian ancestry. In Canada, membership is primarily from Russian Mennonite background.

4
Old Order Churches

Old Order Amish girls in customary dress.

The Mennonites who arrived in Ontario in the 1780s and the Amish who came a few decades later continued for many years to live and worship according to traditions established in Europe. Daily life was devoted to farming and raising large families. Sunday, a day of rest and visiting, began with a solemn worship service consisting of German hymns sung a cappella and in unison, kneeling for silent prayer, and sermons by lay ministers. By the early 1800s, ministers' meetings were laying the foundation for the Mennonite Conference of Ontario. The Amish, meanwhile, continued to worship in homes.

By the 1870s, however, these churches were undergoing dramatic changes. The Mennonite conference introduced Sunday schools, revival meetings, and English gospel songs. Many Amish wanted meetinghouses in which to worship. The changes sparked heated debates between those who were eager to modernize and those who insisted on maintaining old ways.

In the 1880s, the Amish divided into House Amish and Church Amish. The Church Amish changed with the times, formed a conference, and eventually became part of Mennonite Church Canada. The House Amish clung to traditional worship styles and ways of living, and became known as Old Order Amish. In 1889, the Mennonite Conference of Ontario experienced a similar division, with the traditionalists withdrawing and becoming known as Old Order Mennonites.

Essential to the Old Order groups is nonconformity to the world, expressed by plain dress and a way of life outside of society and modern technology. While Old Order groups obey civil law and pay taxes, most do not use government medical care or other programs. Their pacifism is close to the nonresistance ideal of Anabaptism, although Old Orders have, with the help of other Mennonites, successfully petitioned the government to have their own schools and to be exempt from certain legal requirements.

Even Old Order groups change with the times: many now use telephones and some even have computers for farm-based industries. Old Order women sell their wares at the local market and some even run their own businesses. While worship is solemn with unaccompanied German hymns, the young people gather for weekly "singings" to enjoy some lively music and get to know each other.

In 2006, a group of families moved to Manitoba to establish the first Old Order Mennonite settlement outside of Ontario.

Old Order Amish

Members	About 1,500
Congregations (in 13 settlements)	30

Location
Ontario

Schools
29 schools (grades 1-8)

Institutions/Programs
Mutual Aid programs
Pathway Publishers (including
   Heritage Historical Library)

Periodicals
Family Life
The Blackboard Bulletin
Young Companion

History

At the beginning of the Anabaptist-Mennonite movement in the 1500s, Anabaptists in Switzerland and southern Germany were known as Swiss Brethren. In the late 1600s, a Swiss Brethren bishop by the name of Jakob Ammann advocated a stricter discipline to guard against the reabsorption of the Anabaptists into society. He argued that erring members should not only be banned from communion but shunned by church members, a practice that involved discontinuing social interaction such as sharing meals or doing business together. Clothing should be modest, and men's beards untrimmed.

Congregations throughout the Alsace region adopted Ammann's views. Those whom he could not persuade he placed under the ban; the banned group did the same to Ammann and his followers, and the Swiss Brethren divided in 1693. Ammann's group came to be known as the Amish.

The 1700s saw the Amish moving from place to place in Europe as they continued to be persecuted and expelled by civil authorities. As Napoleon began enforcing conscription into his armies, the Amish looked to North America for freedom to practise their faith. In 1822, the first Amish arrived in Ontario, joining the small group that had moved there from the United States.

In the 1880s, the Ontario Amish divided over the decision to build meetinghouses for worship, a symbol of the changes that were happening in the Amish community. Those who continued to meet in homes—the House Amish—maintained traditional ways and came to be known as Old Order Amish. The Church Amish established the Ontario Amish Mennonite Conference in 1923 and then dropped the Amish name altogether in the 1960s when they became the Western Ontario Mennonite Conference. Today this "modernized" Amish wing is part of Mennonite Church Canada.

From 1953 to 1969, a wave of Old Order Amish immigration from Ohio established settlements at Aylmer, Chesley, and other parts of Ontario.

Distinctives

The Amish are the most traditional of all Mennonite groups in Canada. Members worship in homes and still use the *Ausbund*, an Anabaptist German hymnal from the sixteenth century. Pennsylvania Dutch (a Swiss-German dialect) is the main language of home and church, together with some High German. Ministers are chosen by lot. The Amish excommunicate erring members, shunning or avoiding them until they repent or leave the church altogether.

Two distinctives in appearance set the Amish apart from other conservative groups: men wear untrimmed beards with no moustaches, and clothing is usually fastened with hooks and eyes instead of buttons. Both practices began in reaction to military uniforms of the sixteenth century. Amish women wear head coverings and long dresses in dark colours.

Like Old Order Mennonites, the Amish have their own schools and teachers, grades one through eight. (The Ontario government has allowed private, nonsupervised elementary education since 1966.) Higher education is forbidden. Horses are used for farming, and horse-drawn buggies are the means of transportation. For longer trips, Old Order groups hire vans and drivers or take public transportation. Rules on technology, such as use of electricity and telephones, may differ from community to community.

While the Amish pay taxes, they generally reject social security and rely on their own mutual aid programs. Some, however, do use government health programs such as clinic-based prenatal care. Many have property protection with the Amish Mennonite Fire and Storm Aid Union, which dates to 1858, and they bank with the Mennonite Savings and Credit Union. The Amish have a thriving publishing business, Pathway Publishers, based in Aylmer, Ontario, which also serves Old Order Mennonites. Pathway publishes three periodicals, textbooks for Amish and Old Order Mennonite schools, and books in German and English.

Members also read *The Budget* (begun in Ohio in 1890) and *Die Botschaft*, both based on reader correspondence. Pathway's Heritage Historical Library has a rich collection of resources on Old Order Amish and Mennonite groups.

Men and women leave through separate doors after worship at an Old Order Mennonite meetinghouse in Waterloo County, Ontario.

The Detweiler Meetinghouse, built near Kitchener in 1855, is the only surviving stone meeting-house built by Mennonite pioneers in Ontario. The restored interior contains the long pulpit, benches and coat hooks still used in Old Order Mennonite meetinghouses.

Old Order Mennonites

Members	3,780

Congregations	About 31

Location
Ontario, with one in Manitoba

Schools
43 schools, grades 1-8

Institutions/Programs
Mutual aid plan

Periodicals
See Amish publications

History

For the first 100 years of their life in Canada, Mennonites continued to live and worship in the patterns set by previous generations. Congregations were guided by like-minded ministers and bishops within the Mennonite Conference of Ontario.

By the 1870s, Mennonites were experiencing the winds of change. Methodist revivalism was inspiring the Ontario conference to begin Sunday schools and hold revival meetings, to sing gospel songs, and to use more English in worship. Some ordained leaders resisted these changes and expressed alarm at the increasing acceptance of "worldly" ways. Some leaders refused to baptize candidates who were influenced by revivalism.

At the 1887 assembly of the conference, Bishop Abraham Martin and his traditionalist sympathizers engaged the other leaders in a heated discussion, objecting vehemently to modernization and outside influences such as English preaching and Sunday school. After the discussion, they left the meeting. The next year, Martin held a separate assembly at the Martin Meetinghouse just outside of Waterloo. Four ministers and six deacons stood with him.

The final break came in 1889 when Martin and his supporters led their congregations out of the conference. This breakaway group became known as the Old Order Mennonite Church because of its insistence on

91

An Old Order couple heads for home.

maintaining old ways. Located primarily in Waterloo Region, Old Order communities have spread beyond this region in recent decades to escape the encroachment of the city and to find farmland for their children.

At least two independent groups have emerged out of the Old Order Mennonite Church. In 1917, David Martin and his followers established a church that practised more rigorous shunning of excommunicated members. The David Martin group, the most strict and independent of the Old Orders, retains traditional practices such as non-rubber wheels on buggies while allowing cell phones and computers. Some members operate highly skilled, computerized manufacturing industries on their farms, with markets in North America and beyond. The David Martin group has approximately 800 members.

In the early 1950s, Elam S. Martin left the David Martin group and in 1957 formed the Orthodox Mennonite Church. This group has experienced various divisions over the years, with a large portion of members returning to the David Martin group in 1986. Orthodox men wear beards, like the Amish. The Orthodox church now has three congregations in Ontario, with about 350 members. A small breakaway group near Wallenstein has about 10 members. A group that moved to Manitoba in 2006 has approximately 20 members.

Distinctives

Old Order Mennonites are a highly visible minority, with their nineteenth-century dress and horse-and-buggy transportation. Women wear long cape dresses (the "cape" is a fold of fabric over the bust) and white net head coverings. Outer wear consists of black bonnets and shawls. Men wear black pants with suspenders and dark shirts. They are clean shaven (as opposed to Amish men, who wear beards without moustaches). Black frock coats and hats are Sunday dress for men, although young men may be seen in conventional suits and ties.

Members live according to community *Ordnung* (rules of living), which includes an emphasis on humility (*Demut*) and simplicity. Photographs are linked to personal vanity and generally forbidden. Most Old Order members are farmers, using varying degrees of mechanization. Homes are plain, but most by now have electricity. Telephones are now permitted in homes as well.

Worship is held in plain, white meetinghouses, with separate entrances for men and women. Services are a mix of Pennsylvania Dutch and High German, with German hymnbooks. The church is led by ordained ministers and deacons who are chosen by lot from among the men of the congregation. Bishops, chosen from among the ministers, oversee several congregations and officiate at baptisms, ordinations, and communion, as well as weddings and funerals. They are also largely responsible for church discipline, including excommunication of members who do not follow Old Order ways. (Shunning of excommunicated members is not as harsh as among the Amish, except for the David Martin group.)

Old Order Mennonites operate their own schools for grades one through eight, using curriculum published by the Amish. English is the language of instruction, with special classes to learn German. While Old Orders pay taxes, they generally do not participate in any government insurance, pension or health plans. Old folks live with their children.

"Ties that Bind," a copper metal sculpture more than nine feet high, hangs in the atrium of Conrad Grebel University College. Created by Ontario Mennonite artist Jo-Anne Harder, the 41 panels tell the 500-year Mennonite story through images of place, memory, and identity.

94

Markham-Waterloo Mennonite Conference

Members	1,400
Congregations	12

Location
Southern Ontario

Schools
About 7 (shared with Old Order Mennonites)

Institutions/Programs
Mennonite Aid Ordinance
Hospital insurance plan

Publications
The Church Correspondent

History

This conference is the car-driving branch of the Old Order Mennonite community in Ontario. The Old Order Mennonite Church was formed in 1889 when traditionalists left the Ontario Mennonite Conference in order to maintain the old ways of living and worship.

By 1930, Old Order Mennonite communities in Markham and Rainham, Ontario, were permitting cars and telephones and were using English in their worship services. The Old Order Mennonite Church considered these changes to be unacceptable and dissociated itself from these congregations in 1931.

In 1939, a large group in Waterloo County withdrew from the Old Order church, also over use of cars and telephones, and joined with the Markham church to form the Markham-Waterloo Mennonite Conference. While slightly more modernized than their horse-and-buggy cousins, Markham-Waterloo members continue to live and worship in traditional ways.

While the Markham congregation has virtually disappeared, the Markham-Waterloo conference has spread beyond Waterloo County as far as the Ottawa Valley. The conference has ties with the Ohio-Indiana (Wisler) and Weaverland Old Order groups in the United States, including pulpit sharing, but these groups have no structural links. The conference supports inter-Mennonite efforts such as Mennonite Central Committee and the annual Ontario Mennonite Relief Sale in New Hamburg.

Distinctives

Markham-Waterloo Mennonites are distinguished from other Old Order Mennonites primarily by their use of cars and modern technology for farm life. They used to be called "black-bumper Mennonites" because they permitted only black cars with the chrome painted black. Black cars are still the norm, but only the ministers and a few individuals still paint the bumpers black.

In worship, the Markham-Waterloo group maintains Old Order ways. Each congregation is led by a minister and deacon, chosen by lot from among the men of the congregation. Bishops, who oversee several congregations, are chosen from among the ministers. The bishop performs baptisms, ordinations, weddings, and funerals, and officiates at communion. He is also largely responsible for maintaining church discipline.

During worship, members kneel for prayer, and singing is a cappella. Unlike the Old Order Mennonite churches, however, worship in the Markham-Waterloo group is entirely in English. There are no Sunday schools. Youth meet for singings and social events. Dress is conservative, with cape dresses and prayer coverings for women and plain, black clothes for men.

The conference operates several of its own elementary schools and

An Old Order Mennonite family in Kitchener, Ontario.

shares others with Old Order Mennonites. A few children attend public schools. Radio and television are resisted, but many things are left up to individual discretion. Modern technology, such as farm machinery, is generally accepted.

The church's house insurance plan (Mennonite Aid Ordinance) is used by individuals from other Old Order and conservative groups as well; the hospital plan has fallen into disuse because of government medical coverage. About half of the membership uses the financial services of the Mennonite Savings and Credit Union, which serves members of Mennonite, Amish, and Brethren in Christ churches in Ontario.

5
Conservative Churches of Swiss-German Origin

Volunteers in Ontario can meat donated to Mennonite Central Committee for distribution to hungry people around the world.

In the 1950s, Mennonite conferences in Ontario of Swiss and Amish origin were experiencing the stresses of change. Radio and television were entering the home, and musical instruments were entering the church. Women were cutting their hair and putting away their prayer coverings, and young people were going to college and entering professions. Many welcomed the changes, while others felt that the Mennonite doctrine of nonconformity to the world was being severely threatened.

In 1956, a bishop and several members of the Amish Mennonite Conference in Ontario (not to be confused with Old Order Amish) withdrew from their congregation in Millbank to form the Bethel Conservative Mennonite Church. This was the first church to use the conservative name and marks the founding of the Conservative Mennonite movement. The new congregation was joined by people from other Amish and Mennonite churches who were eager to maintain traditional ways.

A recent directory defines Conservative Mennonites this way: "In these days of moral decadence and spiritual apostasy, it is our desire to uphold the doctrines of the Scriptures as historically taught by the Mennonite church; such as separation from the world, nonresistance, separation of church and state, permanence of marriage, the Christian women's veiling, moral purity, and leadership of man" (*Mennonite Church Directory 2005*, Christian Light Publications, Harrisonburg, Virginia).

Conservative Mennonites have kept the plain dress—cape dresses and coverings for women, straight coats for men—and other signs of nonconformity. While radios are tolerated, television is frowned upon. Members do not vote or participate in civil affairs. Conference structures would be considered accommodations to the world, but conservatives do have loosely organized fellowships for mutual support and mission work.

A fascinating development in recent decades is that Russian Mennonites of Low German background are being integrated into Swiss Conservative groups. In Ontario, some Old Colony Mennonites returning from Mexico are joining conservative churches. In western Canada, about a dozen congregations of Old Colony and Kleine Gemeinde background are now part of the Nationwide Mennonite Fellowship. For those familiar with common surnames in the different traditions, it is fascinating to see a Swartzentruber and a Bauman listed alongside a Plett as ministers of a congregation in Manitoba. This union parallels what has taken place in Mennonite Church Canada as these different immigrant groups are finding each other in a Canadian context.

Beachy Amish Mennonite Churches

Members	371
Congregations	10

Location
Ontario

Schools
3 elementary schools
Calvary Bible School in Arkanas

Institutions/Programs
Mission Interests Committee
Amish Mennonite Aid

Periodicals
Calvary Messenger (published in Ohio)

History

In the 1920s, an Amish bishop in Pennsylvania, Moses M. Beachy, decided he could not enforce the Amish practice of shunning those who had been banned from the church for joining other Mennonite groups. Those who favoured the strict ban, about half the congregation, withdrew from Beachy's leadership in 1927 and continued meeting as traditional Amish. The Beachy group and the Amish group, however, continued to share the same meetinghouse for 26 years.

In 1928, when the Beachy group decided to allow cars, the split was complete. The Beachy congregation linked up with the Weavertown Amish church in Pennsylvania, which had also arisen out of disagreement over the ban, to form the Beachy Amish fellowship.

Two Amish Mennonite congregations in Ontario eventually identified with the Beachy Amish movement: the Mornington church, founded in 1904, and the Cedar Grove church, founded in 1911. Today 10 congregations in Ontario identify themselves as Beachy Amish, but there is no formal organization uniting them. Members keep in touch across the U.S. border (there are 108 congregations in the United States) and with mission churches in Central America. Ministers have met annually since 1964, youth since 1953. Beachy Amish in Ontario do not have links with the Old Order Amish.

The 1950s saw considerable growth in

This monument, erected in 1986 to commemorate the 200 years of Mennonite settlement in Canada, stands at the site of the country's oldest Mennonite congregation: The First Mennonite Church in Vineland, Ontario.

numbers and a new missionary fervour. In 1959, the Amish Mission Interests Committee came under the control of the Beachy Amish. It has concentrated on projects in North America, including Indian schools and missions in northern Ontario. The four northern mission churches call themselves "Believers Fellowship," without any Amish designation.

Amish Mennonite Aid resulted from relief work with refugees in West Berlin in the 1950s. Hurricane cleanup and agricultural aid led to the founding of churches in Belize and El Salvador in the 1960s. Churches in Paraguay, Honduras and Costa Rica were established by colonization (Beachy Amish families moving to these countries). There are also Beachy Amish congregations in Belgium, Ireland, Romania, Ukraine, Australia and Kenya.

The Beachy Amish also support Christian Aid Ministries, an agency of Swiss Mennonite conservative churches which distributes material aid and Christian literature to numerous countries around the world, including Ukraine, Liberia and Haiti. Headquarters are in Berlin, Ohio, with a material aid warehouse near Wallenstein, Ontario.

Distinctives

The Beachy Amish have links with Conservative Mennonite churches, and their practices fall somewhere between conservative and Old Order. They use modern appliances and vehicles. Clothing is conservative but more colourful than Old Order groups.

Beachy Amish churches are strongly congregational and have resisted any conference organization. Ministers are selected by lot, and higher education is discouraged. Worship services, in English, are held in meetinghouses, except for some northern congregations that meet in homes. Most congregations have Sunday schools and Bible studies. Bible conferences and revival meetings are common.

Conservative Mennonite Church of Ontario

Members	566

Congregations	9

Location
Ontario, as far north as Rainy River

Schools
8 schools (up to grade 10)

Institutions/Programs
Conservative Mennonite Foreign Missions (work in India)
Conservative Mennonite Automobile Brotherhood Assistance Plan

Periodicals
Ontario Informer

History

In 1959, the Mennonite Conference of Ontario experienced a division over the direction the conference was moving. Six church leaders, led by bishops Moses Roth and Curtis Cressman, could no longer tolerate what they saw as the church's departure from its distinctive historic and biblical faith and practice, especially in regards to nonconformity and spiritual discipline.

The debate over nonconformity illustrated the polarization that was occurring among Ontario Mennonites during the 1950s as the majority moved away from distinctive clothing (cape dresses and prayer coverings for women and plain coats for men) and began to allow radios and other signs of conformity to the culture.

The two bishops withdrew from the conference, taking with them about 7 percent of the membership of the Wilmot area churches. This secessionist group became the Conservative Mennonite Church of Ontario. In 1965, the conservative church began a mission to Ojibwa people in northern Ontario. Together with conservative groups in the United States, the Ontario church supports mission work in other countries, with a particular focus on India since 1981. The Conservative Mennonite Foreign Missions now has three congregations in India.

In 1975, differences over radio use led about a third of the more lenient members to leave and establish the Heidelberg Fellowship

Church, which relates to the Midwest Mennonite Fellowship. Meanwhile, new members have come from the Old Order Mennonite community and, more recently, from Old Colony Russian Mennonites returning to Canada from Mexico. Virtually every congregation now has Mexican Mennonite members, and one congregation has retained the German language for their sake.

The Conservative church relates to other conservative groups in the United States and Canada, especially the Nationwide Fellowship Churches and the Eastern Pennsylvania Mennonite Church. These groups exchange preachers and share Winter Bible School sessions.

Distinctives

Like other conservative groups of Swiss Mennonite background, the Conservative Mennonite Church of Ontario combines evangelical theology with a conservative lifestyle. Women wear cape dresses and white net prayer coverings over uncut hair; men wear plain coats with no lapels. (Women who come from the Old Colony church in Mexico are required to give up their own distinctive dress—dark print dresses and black kerchiefs—when they join this group.) Television and other "worldly entertainments" are frowned upon.

Young women from the Conservative Mennonite Church set up a quilt for auction at the Ontario Mennonite Relief Sale in New Hamburg, one of the largest MCC sales in North America.

Bishops and ministers lead the church, which is active in missions and supports revival meetings and Bible conferences. English is used in home and church. The group operates its own car insurance, with some Markham-Waterloo and Beachy Amish members also participating. A requirement is that the cars have no radios.

The Mennonite Savings and Credit Union, based in Kitchener, Ontario, serves members from most Mennonite groups. It has nine branches across southern Ontario.

Midwest Mennonite Fellowship

Members	884
Congregations	9

Location
Ontario

Schools
4 schools, grades 1-10
Maranatha Bible School
(Minnesota)

Institutions/Programs
Deeper Life Ministries

Periodicals
Midwest Mennonite Focus

The Midwest Mennonite Fellowship is an association of about 30 congregations scattered across North America; the Canadian members are all in Ontario. It goes back to 1977, when congregations in Ontario and several states were looking for a less rigid conservatism. The largest contingent was a group of congregations that had left the Conservative Mennonite Church of Ontario in 1976. The Fellowship established the Maranatha Bible School in Lansing, Minnesota, in 1978.

The largest congregation in Ontario is Countryside Mennonite Fellowship in Hawkesville, with 223 members. While dress remains conservative, congregations have Sunday schools, Bible conferences, and revival meetings. In this they are much like the Nationwide Fellowship Churches; a difference is that the Midwest Fellowship permits radios while the Nationwide Fellowship does not.

The Midwest Mennonite Fellowship supports Maranatha Bible School and Deeper Life Ministries, a counselling program based in Ohio. Many Ontario congregations support Northern Youth Programs, which operates a camp, Bible institute, and high schools for native youth in northwestern Ontario. (Northern Youth Programs was begun by Northern Light Gospel Mission in 1968 and is now operated by the nondenominational Living Hope Native Ministries.) Some congregations also support Eagle Wings Discipleship Ministries, a residential counselling program near Port Elgin, Ontario.

The plain church building of conservative Mennonites in Ontario is very similar to the churches of Russian Mennonite conservatives in western Canada.

Nationwide Fellowship Churches

Members	989
Congregations	23

Location
Alberta: 6 congregations
British Columbia: 3
Manitoba: 4
Nova Scotia: 1
Ontario: 7
Saskatchewan: 2

Schools
21 elementary schools
Messiah Bible School (Ohio)

Institutions/Programs
Philippine Witness

Periodicals
The Harvest Call (published in Ontario)
The Philippine Witness (published in McBride, British Columbia)
Fellowship Newsletter (published in New Mexico)

The Nationwide Fellowship is a loose association of congregations in North America. Its beginnings go back to the conservative movement among Amish and (Swiss) Mennonite churches in Ontario in the 1950s.

In 1957, the Bethel Conservative Church in Ontario, the first to use the "conservative" name, joined with two Ohio congregations to organize the Conservative Mennonite Fellowship. The Bethel church had left the Amish Mennonite Conference because it felt the conference was drifting toward cultural conformity and a structural hierarchy.

In 1958, the Conservative Mennonite Fellowship founded the Messiah Bible School, now located in Carbon Hill, Ohio. It also sent missionaries to Guatemala, beginning in the 1960s. In the early 1990s, the fellowship disbanded, with congregations moving to the Nationwide or Midwest fellowships.

While disaffected churches of the Amish conference were regrouping as conservatives in the 1950s, congregations were leaving the (Swiss) Mennonite Conference of Ontario over similar issues. Ministers from Ontario who wished to maintain conservative dress and a nonconformist lifestyle met with leaders from Pennsylvania and Virginia in 1959 to discuss how they might support each other. These meetings marked the beginning of what is known as the Fellowship Churches or Nationwide Fellowship.

Today, total membership is about 4,000 members in 104 churches across North

America. Members meet regionally for fellowship while maintaining congregational independence. Leaders meet yearly to coordinate their efforts. Mission workers have established churches in Mexico, Guatemala, Dominican Republic, Bolivia, Paraguay, Nigeria, and the Philippines, and in many states. Each regional fellowship focuses on one mission field and publishes a newsletter to keep members informed.

In 1962, some members moved to British Columbia and started a church there. In recent years, Fellowship churches have been established among conservative Russian Mennonites in Manitoba, Saskatchewan, and Alberta. These western churches are grouped regionally under the name Northwest Fellowship. The Conservative Mennonite Church of Ontario was initially a regional group as well. While no longer formally linked, it maintains cordial ties with the Nationwide Fellowship.

The Fellowship churches consider education a scriptural requirement for the preservation of the faith, and most congregations have their own schools. The group supported Rod and Staff Publishers in Kentucky in 1990 in developing a Christian school curriculum for grades one through ten.

Other Conservative Mennonite Groups

The following groups, all based in the United States, have emerged among congregations of Swiss Mennonite and Amish background. In western Canada, however, members are largely of Russian Mennonite background, attracted in recent years by the biblical conservatism and nonconformity of these groups. Many congregations operate their own schools.

Members	22
Congregations	1
(Eden, Manitoba)	

Bethel Fellowship

Based in Missouri, the North American body has 738 members in 18 congregations.

Members	37
Congregations	2
(Raymond, Alberta and Millbank, Ontario)	

Biblical Mennonite Alliance

Formed in 1998 in Ohio, this alliance has a total of 1,993 members in 39 congregations.

Members	57
Congregations	1
(Red Lake, Ontario)	

Conservative Mennonite Conference

Of Amish origin, this conference has 113 congregations with 11,000 members in 24 states and Mexico. It is based in Rosedale, Ohio.

Members	195
Congregations	4
(all in northern British Columbia: 2 in Burns Lake, 1 in Montney, and 1 in Vanderhoof)	

Eastern Pennsylvania Mennonite Church

These congregations emerged from a mission effort to native people in northern British Columbia. Members come largely, however, from Swiss and Russian Mennonite groups. North American membership is 4,767 members in 68 congregations, mostly in Pennsylvania.

Members	141
Congregations	2
(Ontario)	

Members	116
Congregations	2
(North Easthope and Stevensville, Ontario)	

Members	54
Congregations	1
(Raymond Alberta)	

Members	About 450
Congregations	11

Maranatha Amish Mennonite Churches

Based in Pennsylvania, the North American body has a total of 8 congregations. It grew out of the Beachy Amish.

Reformed Mennonite Church

John Herr founded this group in Pennsylvania in 1812 to reestablish the true church of Menno Simons. He organized churches in Ontario beginning in 1833. While emphasizing nonconformity, the group has no Sunday school and permits its youth to participate fully in society until baptism. Membership has dwindled dramatically in recent years, with a few congregations left in the United States.

Western Conservative Mennonite Fellowship

Based in Oregon, this group has a total of 12 congregations, plus 2 mission churches in Belize.

Unaffiliated congregations

2 in Alberta, 1 in Manitoba, 8 in Ontario

6
Related Groups

Volunteer Don Burkhardt knots quilts at the MCC Ontario material aid centre. Besides making blankets for needy people around the world, many Mennonites volunteer in MCC thrift shops where sale of used clothing and other items has raised more than $100 million since 1972, when the first store opened in Altona, Manitoba.

The two groups included in this section are related to Mennonites in very different ways. The Brethren in Christ Church has much in common with the Mennonite church, particularly in its commitment to pacifism and service. This has led to partnerships in peace and service efforts through Mennonite Central Committee and other organizations. Brethren in Christ churches are also members of Mennonite World Conference, working together with Mennonite churches around the globe.

The Hutterian Brethren, or Hutterites, while sharing Anabaptist origins with Mennonites, have developed a distinctive and independent way of life. Hutterites are the only Anabaptist group to maintain a truly communal lifestyle; they live in self-sufficient colonies where they manage to hold together traditional customs with state-of-the-art agribusiness. They continue to define themselves by their Anabaptist roots.

A number of other groups in Canada are linked to Mennonites historically but no longer identify with the name. For example, the 1990 edition of this book included the Native Mennonite Conference, renamed the Christian Anishinabec Fellowship in 1996. That fellowship emerged from the Northern Light Gospel Mission, a Mennonite ministry based in Red Lake, Ontario. This mission to northern Ontario native groups, more recently known as Impact North Ministries, has been supported by Ontario Mennonites over the years. As of 2007, Impact North is in the process of disbanding and handing its work over to Living Hope Native Ministries, a nondenominational ministry also based in Red Lake. The Christian Anishinabec Fellowship no longer exists, but Living Hope will continue some of its activities.

A group called Charity Ministries, based in Lancaster, Pennsylvania, includes seven Canadian congregations in four provinces. Formed in 1982 of Old Order and Beachy Amish members, this cluster of independent congregations now includes people from Old Colony and Conservative Mennonite background. Charity Ministries does not identify itself as Mennonite but does "support much of the conservative Mennonite doctrine," according to one member. Revivalist in orientation, it sponsors an outreach ministry of gospel tapes.

The Fellowship of Evangelical Bible Churches, with 22 congregations in five provinces, was formerly known as the Evangelical Mennonite Brethren Conference. Founded in 1889 by Mennonite immigrants from Russia, the group has dropped its Mennonite identity and adopted its current name in

1987. The new name reflects "a renewed desire to be actively involved in evangelism and church planting in North America," according to one leader, who noted that members "adhere faithfully to belief in the inspiration, inerrancy, and authority of the Bible as God's Word."

Another denomination with historic connections to Mennonites is the Evangelical Missionary Church of Canada. The result of a merger in 1993, this group

The Mennonite Trust office in Saskatchewan, part of a financial services company that began in Waldenheim, Saskatchewan, in 1917. It is now a partnership among Mennonite Church Saskatchewan, the Saskatchewan Conference of Mennonite Brethren Churches, and the Fellowship of Evangelical Bible Churches.

includes the former Missionary Church, which emerged from a revival movement within Swiss Mennonite and Brethren in Christ groups in the late nineteenth century. That movement, which drew churches in Canada and the United States, was known as the Mennonite Brethren in Christ Church until 1947. In 1987, the Missionary Church of Canada became independent from its U.S. counterpart and six years later merged with the Evangelical Church of Canada.

In the United States, the Missionary Church has taken a renewed interest in its Anabaptist roots and has initiated contacts with Mennonite Church USA and Mennonite World Conference. In 1997, the Missionary Church in India, which has maintained Mennonite connections, helped host the Mennonite World Conference Assembly. The Evangelical Missionary Church of Canada is a member of the Mennonite Foundation of Canada. It is also a member of the Canadian Foodgrains Bank, an interdenominational food aid organization founded by Mennonite Central Committee Canada in 1983.

The Meeting House, a Brethren in Christ movement with six locations in urban Ontario, bills itself as "a church for people who aren't into church." Its services attract thousands of worshippers.

Brethren in Christ Church Canadian Conference

Members	**3,240**
Congregations	**43**

Location
Ontario: 39 congregations
Saskatchewan: 4 congregations

Canadian office
416-1 North Service Road E
Oakville, ON L6H 5R2

Schools
Relates to Niagara Christian
  Community of Schools (K-12)

Institutions/Programs
Camp Kahquah, Ontario

Periodicals
BicLink newsletter
Seek magazine (North America
  conference)
Shalom quarterly (North America)

History

The Brethren in Christ Church began around 1778 in Lancaster County, Pennsylvania. The founding families, who came from Anabaptist backgrounds, were deeply affected by the Wesleyan revivals of the eighteenth century, as well as the Pietist movement spread in America by the Moravians and German Baptists. These revivals emphasized a deeply personal conversion experience.

The earliest Brethren in Christ called themselves simply "the Brethren." Outsiders often referred to them as River Brethren, since they lived along the Susquehanna River.

In 1788, a group of Brethren moved to Ontario, where they became known as the "Tunkers" (from the German "to dip") because they practised immersion baptism. The group expressed its faith in ways very similar to Mennonites at the time: avoidance of worldly activities such as amusements and politics, simple dress and lifestyle, a communal identity separate from the world. Their manner of meeting symbolized the concept of brotherhood. For most of the first 100 years, worship services were held in the homes of members. Church buildings were called meetinghouses, as in the Swiss Mennonite tradition, being simple structures with pews on three sides and an unelevated pulpit.

At the time of the Civil War in the United States, the Brethren decided to register themselves under the name Brethren in Christ. In

The Niagara Christian Community of Schools, a Christian private school within the Ontario public school system, maintains ties with the Brethren in Christ conference, which founded it.

1879, the U.S. and Canadian churches formed a General Conference, which gave overall guidance to the regional churches and enabled outreach programs. In 1894 home-mission work started in Chicago, and in 1898 the first foreign mission work began in Rhodesia (now Zimbabwe). Today, Brethren in Christ churches can be found in more than 23 countries around the world.

Most of the Canadian conference churches are located in Ontario. Families migrated to Saskatchewan in 1907 and established several churches there. In 1931, Ontario congregations founded the Ontario Bible School, which later became Niagara Christian College, a high school in Fort Erie. This school, now expanded to include kindergarten through grade 12 and renamed the Niagara Christian Community of Schools, operates as a private institution within the public school system. It maintains ties with the Brethren in Christ church through board membership and a covenant.

Distinctives

The church's statement of faith includes an emphasis on the inspiration of the Holy Spirit, a scriptural focus on piety and obedience, and the importance of community. Personal conversion, including the conversion of children, is emphasized. Distinctives such as a dress code or plain meetinghouses have disappeared, and the group has moved away from radical holiness teaching. Like Mennonites, Brethren in Christ are pacifists and share the Mennonite story of conscientious objection and peacemaking.

The Canadian conference is led by a bishop and a Leadership Team or board of directors. Its programs include youth ministry, a women's organization, church development, missions, and compassionate ministries. Pastors are salaried and appointed through local committees and the bishop. The Brethren in Christ Church is a member of Mennonite World Conference and a partner in Mennonite Central Committee.

Hutterite school girls relax in the hayloft of a Saskatchewan colony.

Hutterian Brethren

Members	**About 30,000**
(including children)	

Congregations	**339**

Location
Alberta: 170 (101 Dariusleut,
  69 Lehrerleut)
British Columbia: 2 (Dariusleut)
Manitoba: 105 (Schmiedeleut)
Saskatchewan: 62 (31 Dariusleut,
  31 Lehrerleut)

History

The Hutterian Brethren, also called Hutterites, is a branch of Anabaptists that, like the Mennonites and Amish, has roots in the Reformation of the sixteenth century. Soon after the movement began in 1525, Anabaptists living in the Austrian Tyrol fled to Moravia (now eastern Czech Republic) to escape persecution.

In 1533, the Anabaptists in Moravia broke into three groups. Those who followed Jakob Hutter's leadership became known as Hutterites. Hutter's group was distinctive because of its communal lifestyle, holding all thing in common, based on New Testament passages such as Acts 2–5 and 2 Corinthians. Hutter died a martyr's death in the Tyrol in 1536.

The Hutterites flourished in Moravia and Slovakia for over a century, developing a strong sense of identity and a rich literature, devotional and historical. The Thirty Years War (1618-48) brought the Moravian colonies to an end. Renewed persecution forced the colonists to flee to Transylvania (now Romania). Down to a handful of members, the Hutterites were joined in the mid-1700s by Lutheran immigrants who were attracted by this form of Christian communism. Persecution, mainly by Jesuits, quickly set in here too. In 1767, the Hutterites fled again, eventually settling in Ukraine near the Mennonites there.

In Ukraine, the Hutterites abandoned communal living for several decades, but leaders reestablished the tradition in 1859. In 1870, the threat of universal military conscription and a "Russification" of culture pressed the Hutterites, along with many Mennonites, to move to North America.

All the Hutterites moved to the United States. The three settlements in South Dakota still define the three Hutterite divisions: the *Dariusleut* (after leader Darius Walter; *leut* means "people"), *Schmiedeleut* (after leader Michael Waldner, a *Schmied*, or blacksmith), and *Lehrerleut* (after leader Jacob Wipf, a *Lehrer*, or teacher).

World War I saw a number of Hutterite men imprisoned for their refusal to bear arms; they suffered great hardship in U.S. prisons and two men died. At that point, 17 of the 18 colonies decided to move to Canada, where exemption from military service was granted. They settled in southern Alberta and Manitoba, and later in Saskatchewan. Today, about three quarters of the colonies are in Canada.

In 1920, a "neo-Hutterian" communal group called the Bruderhof was established in Germany. Founder Eberhard Arnold forged links with North American Hutterites in the 1930s. With war looming in the late 1930s, the pacifist Bruderhof communities moved to England and later to Paraguay and the United States. The Bruderhof movement was officially united with the Hutterites for a brief time in the 1950s and from 1974 to 1990. Continuing conflicts over religious and social differences led the more traditional Dariusleut and Lehrerleut to excommunicate the Bruderhof (*Arnoldleut*) in 1990.

In 1992, the Schmiedeleut experienced a bitter division revolving around the leadership of Jacob Kleinsasser of Manitoba. Colonies were torn apart, and conflicts over financial management ended up in court. About a third of the group remained with Kleinsasser and continued relating to the Bruderhof group. In 1995, the Bruderhof and Hutterites severed all links.

According to a Hutterite website (Hutterites.org), there are about 460 colonies in North America, with about 45,000 members, including children. There is also one colony in Japan listed with the Dariusleut.

Distinctives

The communal lifestyle of the Hutterites sets them apart from all other Anabaptist groups. Each colony, with 10 to 20 families, functions as a collective: the colony owns everything and operates like a corporation, run by the male members. While farming is the main occupation, some colonies also operate manufacturing industries. The colonies own large tracts of land and state-of-the-art equipment. The colony's manager is the elected minister, or Servant of the Word.

Over the years, some provinces have attempted to curb the expansion of colonies, and there have been conflicts with neighbouring farmers. Recent years have seen economic challenges as farm prices drop and young people leave.

Families have their own sleeping quarters but all meals are in common. Each adult has his or her task to perform within the collective. Colony schools are often staffed by teachers from outside. Some students, particularly among the Schmiedeleut, now go on to high school and university, especially to train as teachers. Brandon University in Manitoba offers a Hutterite education program, and Canadian Mennonite University has offered courses for Hutterites.

Hutterites speak a Tyrolean dialect and wear distinctive dress: women wear print dresses with aprons and polka-dot kerchiefs; men wear dark pants and suspenders, and married men usually wear beards. Colonies differ on the use of radio and computers, but television is forbidden. Singing together is central to community life, and instruments are allowed in some Schmiedeleut colonies.

These Hutterite teachers attended a summer class at Menno Simons College in Winnipeg, part of Canadian Mennonite University.

The Schmiedeleut set up their own mutual insurance in 1980. The other two groups depend on inter-colony aid when fire or disaster strikes. The colonies all participate in provincial health plans. They contribute financially to local charities and to Mennonite Disaster Service.

Appendix 1
Summary of Membership in Canada (2006)

Name of Group	Members	Congregations
Canadian Conf. of Mennonite Brethren Churches	36,843	248
Mennonite Church Canada	33,464	224
Independent congregations (former MC Canada)	2,010	13
Evangelical Mennonite Conference	7,341	59
Evangelical Mennonite Mission Conference	4,294	29
Chortitzer Mennonite Conference	1,700	13
Northwest Mennonite Conference	1,100	14
Bergthaler Mennonite Church of Saskatchewan	846	6
Sommerfelder Mennonite Church	5,014	13
Reinland Mennonite Church	3,000	7
Friedensfelder Mennonite Church	25	1
Old Colony Mennonite churches	9,044	21
New Reinland Mennonite Church	250	1
Reinland Mennonite Fellowship Church	975	3
Kleine Gemeinde churches	726	8
Church of God in Christ, Mennonite	4,664	52
Independent conservative churches	1,000	12 (estimate)
Old Order Amish	1,500	30
Old Order Mennonites	3,780	31
Markham-Waterloo Mennonite Conference	1,400	12
Beachy Amish Mennonite Church	371	10
Conservative Mennonite Church of Ontario	566	9
Midwest Mennonite Fellowship	884	9
Nationwide Fellowship Churches	989	23
Other conservative groups	1,015	24
Total	**122,801**	**872**

Appendix 2
Mennonite Membership by Province

Province	Members
Alberta	12,381
British Columbia	25,034
Manitoba	37,853
Ontario	35,714
Quebec	607
Saskatchewan	10,639
New Brunswick	233
Nova Scotia	397
Total	**122,858**

Appendix 3
Mennonites in the 2001 Canadian Census

Province	Population	% of Total Population
Ontario	60,595	0.5%
Manitoba	51,540	4.7%
British Columbia	35,490	0.9%
Alberta	22,785	0.8%
Saskatchewan	19,570	2.0%
Nova Scotia	790	
Quebec	425	
New Brunswick	155	
Prince Edward Island	10	
Newfoundland/Labrador	10	
Northwest Territories	50	
Yukon	40	
Nunavut	10	
Total	**191,470**	**0.6%**

Another 20,590 Canadians identified themselves as Brethren in Christ, a group related to Mennonites. Religion statistics were not part of the 2006 Census but will be collected again in 2011.

Appendix 4
Canadian Mennonite Family Tree

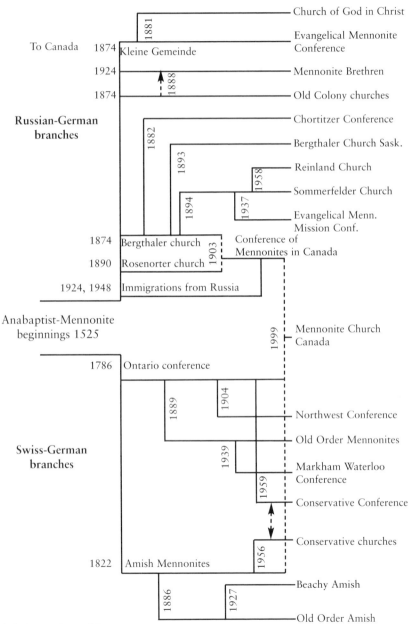

Credit: Margaret Loewen Reimer

128

Appendix 5
Mennonite Organizations

General

Canadian Mennonite Health Assembly
200 Boullee St., New Hamburg, ON N3B 2K4
(An organization of Mennonite healthcare institutions and agencies)

Christian Aid Ministries
3260 Bricker School Line, Route 3, Wallenstein, ON N0B 2S0
(Material aid and literature agency of Beachy Amish and Conservative Mennonites in Ontario.)

MAX Canada Insurance Company
140 Foundry Street, Baden, ON N3A 2P7
(Insurance services for members of the Anabaptist community)

Mennonite Camping Association
North American office: Box 1245, Elkhart, IN 46515-1245
(Includes 12 out of approximately 35 Mennonite camps in Canada)

Mennonite Central Committee (MCC) Canada
134 Plaza Drive, Winnipeg, MB R3T 5K9
(A relief and development agency with provincial organizations and participation in MCC international)

Mennonite Disaster Service
Canadian office: 306 - 2265 Pembina Hwy., Winnipeg, MB R3T 5J3
(A service agency that recruits volunteers for cleanup and rebuilding after disasters)

Mennonite Economic Development Associates
Canadian office: 155 Frobisher Dr., Suite I-106, Waterloo, ON N2V 2E1
(An organization of business people and others with programs in many countries)

Mennonite Foundation of Canada
12 - 1325 Markham Road, Winnipeg, MB R3T 4J6
(Manages investments for charity and provides stewardship education for churches)

Mennonite Historical Society of Canada
1310 Taylor Ave., Winnipeg, MB R3M 3Z6
(Chapters in British Columbia, Alberta, Saskatchewan, Manitoba, Ontario)

Mennonite World Conference
Canadian office: 50 Kent Ave., Kitchener, ON N2G 3R1
Head office: 8, rue du Fossé des Treize, 67000 Strasbourg, France

Ten Thousand Villages Canada
65B Heritage Drive, New Hamburg, ON N3A 2J3
(A fair-trade organization that sells crafts from artisans around the world)

Canadian Foodgrains Bank
400-280 Smith St., Winnipeg, MB R3C 2L4
(An interdenominational food aid organization that includes Mennonite Central Committee Canada.)

Archives

Centre for Mennonite Brethren Studies
1310 Taylor Ave., Winnipeg, MB R3M 3Z6

Heritage Historical Library, Pathway Publishers
Route 4, Aylmer, ON N5H 2R3

Mennonite Archives of Ontario
Conrad Grebel University College, Waterloo, ON N2L 3G6

Mennonite Heritage Centre
600 Shaftesbury Blvd., Winnipeg, MB R3P 0M4

Regional Mennonite Organizations

Financial institutions
Amish Mennonite Fire and Storm Aid Union, Wellesley, Ontario
Mennonite Mutual Insurance Company (Alberta) Ltd., Calgary, Alberta
Mennonite Savings and Credit Union, Kitchener, Ontario
(Mennonite Mutual Fire Insurance Company, Waldheim, Saskatchewan, is a public insurer)

Health and service agencies (a sample)
Eden Health Care Services, Winkler, Manitoba
Edmonton Mennonite Centre for Newcomers, Edmonton, Alberta
Maison de l'Amitié de Montréal, Montreal, Quebec
Supportive Care Services, Abbotsford, British Columbia

Mennonite Schools

Primary and secondary
Canadian Association of Mennonite Schools (CAMS) includes the following primary and secondary schools:
    Menno Simons Christian School, Calgary, Alberta (K-9)
    Mennonite Brethren Collegiate Institute, Winnipeg, Manitoba (7-12)
    Mennonite Collegiate Institute, Gretna, Manitoba (residential, 9-12)
    Mennonite Educational Institute, Abbotsford, British Columbia (K-12)

Rockway Mennonite Collegiate, Kitchener, Ontario (6-12)
Rosthern Junior College, Rosthern, Saskatchewan (residential, 10-12)
Steinbach Christian High School, Steinbach, Manitoba (9-12)
United Mennonite Educational Institute, Leamington, Ontario (9-12)
Westgate Mennonite Collegiate, Winnipeg, Manitoba (7-12)
Winnipeg Mennonite Elementary Schools, Manitoba (K-8, K-6)

Old Order and Conservative Mennonite churches operate hundreds of parochial schools across the country, using their own curriculum and teachers.

Post-secondary
Bethany College, Hepburn, Saskatchewan
Canadian Mennonite University, Winnipeg, Manitoba
Columbia Bible College, Abbotsford, British Columbia
Conrad Grebel University College, University of Waterloo, Ontario
Toronto Mennonite Theological Centre, Toronto (teaching centre of Conrad Grebel University College at the Toronto School of Theology)
École de Théologie Évangélique de Montréal, Quebec
Steinbach Bible College, Steinbach, Manitoba

Seminaries
Associated Mennonite Biblical Seminary, Elkhart, Indiana (partnership of Mennonite Church Canada and Mennonite Church USA)
Mennonite Brethren Biblical Seminary, Fresno, California (partnership of Canadian Conference of Mennonite Brethren Churches and U.S. Conference of Mennonite Brethren Churches)

Seminary Partnerships
ACTS (Associated Canadian Theological Schools) located at Trinity Western University in British Columbia, a partnership between Mennonite Brethren Biblical Seminary and faculty from Baptist, Alliance, Free Church, and Pentecostal traditions
Winnipeg Centre for Ministry Studies (partnership of Canadian Mennonite University, Steinbach Bible College, Associated Mennonite Biblical Seminary and Mennonite Brethren Biblical Seminary, and five conferences: Mennonite Church Manitoba, Manitoba Conference of Mennonite Brethren Churches, Evangelical Mennonite Conference, Evangelical Mennonite Mission Conference, and Chortitzer Mennonite Conference)

Appendix 6
Mennonites Around the World

Continent	Country	Members	Total
Africa			529, 703
(19 countries)	Rep. of Congo	216,268	
	Ethiopia	130,731	
North America			499,664
(2 countries)	United States	368,280	
	Canada	131,384	
Asia/Pacific			241,420
(14 countries)	India	146,095	
	Indonesia	72,624	
Central/South America			155,531
and Caribbean (24 countries)	Paraguay	29,461	
	Mexico	25,958	
Europe			52,222
(15 countries)	Germany	32,776	
	Netherlands	10,200	
Total			**1,478,540**

These statistics were compiled by Mennonite World Conference in 2006. This table gives the number of countries in each continent that have Mennonite and Brethren in Christ churches, and shows the two countries with the largest membership. The statistics represent 217 organized church bodies; not all are members of Mennonite World Conference. Groups are included if they are rooted in the Anabaptist-Mennonite stream of church history or have fellowship with churches that are so rooted. For more details, visit the Mennonite World Conference website at www.mwc-cmm.org.

Bibliography

General Resources

Epp, Frank. *Mennonites in Canada 1786-1920* (Vol. 1). Toronto: MacMillan of Canada, 1974.

———. *Mennonites in Canada 1920-1940* (Vol. 2). Toronto: MacMillan of Canada, 1982.

Regehr, T. D. *Mennonites in Canada 1939-1970* (Vol. 3). Toronto: University of Toronto Press, 1996.

Dyck, Cornelius J. *An Introduction to Mennonite History*. Waterloo: Herald Press, 1993.

Global Anabaptist Mennonite Encyclopedia Online: www.gameo.org

Global Mennonite History Series. John Lapp and Arnold Snyder, eds. *Anabaptist Songs in African Hearts: Africa* and *Testing Faith and Tradition: Europe*. Kitchener: Pandora Press and Intercourse: Good Books, 2006. (Volumes on North America, Latin America and Asia to follow.)

Loewen, Harry and Steven Nolt. *Through Fire and Water: An Overview of Mennonite History*. Waterloo: Herald Press, 1996.

Mennonite Encyclopedia, The. Scottdale: Mennonite Publishing House, 1955, 1990.

Snyder, C. Arnold. *Anabaptist History and Theology: An Introduction*. Kitchener: Pandora Press, 1995.

———. *From Anabaptist Seed*. Kitchener: Pandora Press, 1999.

Specific Groups

Ens, Adolf. *Becoming a National Church: A History of the Conference of Mennonites in Canada*. Winnipeg: CMU Press, 2004.

Gingerich, Orland. *The Amish of Canada*. Waterloo: Conrad Press, 1972.

Heppner, Jack. *Search for Renewal: The Story of the Rudner-weider/Evangelical Mennonite Mission Conference 1937-1987*. Winnipeg: Evangelical Mennonite Mission Conference, 1987.

Hofer, Samuel. *The Hutterites: Lives and Images of a Communal People*. Saskatoon: Hofer Publishers, 1998.

Hostetler, John. *Hutterite Society*. Baltimore: The Johns Hopkins University Press, 1974.

Horst, Isaac R. *A Separate People: An Insider's View of Old Order Mennonite Customs and Traditions*. Waterloo: Herald Press, 2000.

Bibliography

Introduction to the Church of God in Christ, Mennonite, An. (See www.bibleviews.com/holdeman.html.)

Kroeker, Wally. *An Introduction to the Russian Mennonites.* Intercourse, Pa.: Good Books, 2005.

Martin, Donald. *Old Order Mennonites of Ontario: Gelassenheit, Discipleship, Brotherhood.* Kitchener: Pandora Press, 2003.

Plett, Harvey. *Seeking to be Faithful: The Story of the Evangelical Mennonite Conference.* Steinbach: The Evangelical Mennonite Conference, 1996.

Regehr, T. D. *Faith, Life and Witness in the Northwest, 1903-2003.* Kitchener: Pandora Press, 2003.

Scott, Stephen. *An Introduction to Old Order and Conservative Mennonite Groups.* Intercourse, Pa: Good Books, 1996.

Sider, E. Morris. *Reflections on a Heritage: Defining the Brethren in Christ.* Grantham, Pa.: Brethren in Christ Historical Society, 1999.

Toews, John B. *A Pilgrimage of Faith: The Mennonite Brethren Church, 1860-1990.* Winnipeg: Kindred Press, 1993.

Toews, Paul, and Kevin Enns-Rempel, eds. *For Everything a Season: Mennonite Brethren in North America, 1874-2002.* Fresno: Historical Commission, 2002.

Additional Resources

Biographies of leaders, such as *Vicarious Pioneer: The Life of Jacob Y. Shantz* by Samuel Steiner, and *J. J. Thiessen: A Leader for His Time* by Esther Epp-Tiessen.

Community and regional profiles, such as *Mennonites in Ontario* by Marlene Epp.

Congregational histories, some of which include extensive community history, such as *Frontier Community to Urban Congregation: First Mennonite Church, Kitchener 1813-1988* by E. Reginald Good, and *The Days of Our Years: A History of the Eigenheim Mennonite Church Community, 1892-1992* by Walter Klaassen.

Studies by Mennonite sociologists such as Leo Driedger and Winfield Fretz, and church historians such as John J. Friesen, Royden Loewen, and Rodney Sawatsky.

Studies on church music by musicologists such as Wesley Berg and Doreen Klassen, and the "Mennonite" entry in the *Encyclopedia of Music in Canada* (available online).

Theological works such as *The Politics of Jesus* by John Howard Yoder and *Mennonites and Classical Theology* by A. James Reimer.

Sample of Canadian Mennonite Literature

Sandra Birdsell, *The Rüssländer* (2002). A novel about a Mennonite community caught in the Russian Revolution.

Mabel Dunham, *Trail of the Conestoga* (1924). The story of an 1802 Mennonite migration from Pennsylvania to Ontario.

Patrick Friesen, *The Shunning* (1980). A group of poems about a man's exclusion from the church.

Ingrid Rimland, *The Wanderers* (1977). A gripping novel about a family's life in South America and Canada.

Barbara Smucker, *Henry's Red Sea* (1955), *Days of Terror* (1979), *Amish Adventure* (1983). Stories for older children about the Mennonite experience.

Hildi Froese Tiessen, ed., *Liars and Rascals* (1989). An anthology of Mennonite short stories.

Miriam Toews, *A Complicated Kindness* (2004). A tragic-comic novel about a teenager in a repressive Mennonite community.

Armin Wiebe, *The Salvation of Yasch Siemens* (1984). A rollicking story set in a Low German Manitoba community.

Rudy Wiebe, *Peace Shall Destroy Many* (1962), *The Blue Mountains of China* (1970), *Sweeter Than All the World* (2002). Novels by a chronicler of the Russian Mennonite tradition.

Well-known Mennonite poets include Di Brandt, Patrick Friesen, Sarah Klassen, Barbara Nickel, and David Waltner-Toews.

Photo Credits

Page 25: Photo by Terrance Klassen.
Page 26: Conrad Grebel University College
Page 27: Photo by Mike Wiebe
Page 28 top: Killarney Park Mennonite Brethren Church
Page 28 bottom: Columbia Bible College
Page 30: *Canadian Mennonite*
Page 31: Waterloo Mennonite Brethren Church
Page 36: *Canadian Mennonite*
Page 37: *Canadian Mennonite*
Page 38: Aiden Schlichting Enns
Page 39: Canadian Mennonite University
Page 40: Mennonite Church Manitoba
Page 43: Gladys Terichow
Page 44: Steinbach Bible College
Page 46: *The Messenger*
Page 48: *The Messenger*
Page 50: *EMMC Recorder*
Page 51: *EMMC Recorder*
Page 53: MCC
Page 54: *The Chronicle*
Page 56: *The Chronicle*
Page 57: *The Chronicle*
Page 58 top and bottom: Northwest Mennonite Conference
Page 61: MCC photo by Joanie Peters
Page 65: *Canadian Mennonite*
Page 66: Aiden Schlichting Enns
Page 69: *Canadian Mennonite*
Page 70: Ken Loewen
Page 72: *Canadian Mennonite*
Page 74: Byron Rempel-Burkholder
Page 77: MCC photo by Joanie Peters
Page 82: *Canadian Mennonite*
Page 85: Hunsberger Photography
Page 89: Hunsberger Photography
Page 90: Gerald Musselman
Page 92: Mennonite Archives of Ontario

Photo Credits

Page 94: *Canadian Mennonite*
Page 96: Mennonite Archives of Ontario
Page 99: Ross Muir
Page 102: *Mennonite Reporter*
Page 104: MCC photo by Carl Hiebert
Page 106: Mennonite Savings and Credit Union
Page 108: *Canadian Mennonite*
Page 113: MCC photo by Melissa Engel
Page 115: Karin Fehderau
Page 116: Brethren in Christ Church
Page 118: Brethren in Christ Church
Page 120: Burton Buller
Page 123: *Canadian Mennonite*

The Author

 Margaret Loewen Reimer was associate editor of the *Mennonite Reporter* from 1973 to 1997 and managing editor of its successor, the *Canadian Mennonite*, until 2005. She has led numerous workshops for writers and lectured in various settings on theology and the arts. She has also written articles for many other church periodicals and literary journals. Margaret was born in Altona, Manitoba, and lives in Waterloo, Ontario. She and her husband, Jim, have three children and two grandchildren. They are members of Rockway Mennonite Church in Kitchener, Ontario.